How to Invest
$50–$5,000

W9-BRG-742

HOW TO INVEST $50–$5,000

Sixth Edition

NANCY DUNNAN

HarperPerennial
A Division of HarperCollins*Publishers*

HOW TO INVEST $50–$5,000 *(Sixth Edition)*. Copyright © 1997 by Cloverdale Press, Inc. All rights reserved. Printed in the United States of America. No part of this book may be used or reproduced in any manner whatsoever without written permission except in the case of brief quotations embodied in critical articles and reviews. For information address HarperCollins Publishers, Inc., 10 East 53rd Street, New York, New York 10022.

HarperCollins books may be purchased for educational, business, or sales promotional use. For information, please write to: Special Markets Department, HarperCollins Publishers, Inc., 10 East 53rd Street, New York, New York 10022.

FIRST EDITION

Library of Congress Cataloging-in-Publication Data
Dunnan, Nancy.
    How to invest $50–$5,000 / Nancy Dunnan. — 6th ed.
        p. cm.
    Includes index.
    ISBN 0-06-273479-2
    1. Investments—Handbooks, manuals, etc. I. Title.
    HG4527.D767 1997
    332.67'8—dc21   96–40392

97 98 99 00 ◆/RRD 10 9 8 7 6 5 4 3

Contents

INTRODUCTION

Getting the Most for Your Money

A fool and his money are soon parted.

—English proverb

This book is intended to help you keep your money, whether you have just a few dollars or a few thousand. It seems as though most people, no matter how much money they make, really don't know how to save—or even if they do save, they don't know what to do with their savings. So, they and their money soon part ways.

Not a good thing.

This book is for you if. . .

- You're a new or small investor.
- You have money sitting in an account somewhere earning less than 4 percent interest.
- You're just starting out on your first job.
- You've saved several hundred dollars from your summer work.
- You have put aside several thousand dollars from careful budgeting.
- You received a sudden windfall so that for the first time in your life you have a lump sum to invest.
- You were handed a nice bonus at work.
- You have a business that's taking off.

So, no matter what your circumstances, I encourage you to start to save and invest right now—today. For the sooner you begin, the sooner your $50, $500, or $5,000 will grow and grow, so that eventually you can hand over this book to someone else.

Please don't wait until your next raise, until next year, or until next anything. Waiting only means you'll never get started.

Never Too Little

Sometimes investors feel they don't have enough money to invest, that their options are limited. I'm here to tell you they're not. More than two dozen investment choices are described in this book.

You'll learn how to take advantage of each one. In fact, you'll soon discover that all the financial world is wooing you and your money: banks, brokerage firms, mutual fund companies, and financial planners are vying for your cash—be it $50 or $5,000.

REACHING YOUR GOALS—HOW SAVING CAN BE FUN

Your personal financial goals will vary throughout your life, depending upon your age, your income, and your interests. The best way to reach any goal is to write it down, assign it a target date, and figure out how much you need to save to accomplish your dream. Here's a fill-in worksheet you can use as a model. Add your own particular spin to it.

Goal	Cost	Target Date	Months to Go	Save Each Month
Degree	_____	_____	_____	$_____
Car	_____	_____	_____	_____
Computer	_____	_____	_____	_____
Vacation	_____	_____	_____	_____
House	_____	_____	_____	_____
New kitchen	_____	_____	_____	_____
Collectible	_____	_____	_____	_____
Start business	_____	_____	_____	_____

By the time you're halfway through this book, you'll be comfortable moving your money around from one investment to another as your needs change, as interest rates rise and fall, and as you earn more and more money.

Remember: The right place for your first $50 won't be the right one for your first $500 or $5,000—no one investment weathers all economic storms.

The Learning Process

Being a good investor does take some time and knowledge. If you follow my step-by-step plan—starting with $50—you'll soon know exactly what to do and when. I urge you to set aside some time to learn about handling your money, to explore the world of finance. Listen to the business news; read about it in newspapers, magazines, or on-line. Do so for one very simple reason: No one cares as much about your money as you do! No one.

Begin by reading the box that follows called The Ten Dumbest Mistakes People Make About Money. You'll soon see you're not alone in shying away from investing, in putting off saving.

Second, put a check next to those mistakes that are yours.

Third, reread my solutions for each mistake. They are simple and easy to follow.

Fourth and finally, resolve to take action today—or at least before the end of the month!

THE RULE OF 72

A quick way to calculate how long it will take you to double your investment—at any interest rate—is to use "The Rule of 72." **Divide 72 by the interest rate and you wind up with the number of years it will take to double your money**.
For example:
72 divided by 3 ½ percent is 24 years
72 divided by 6 percent is 12 ½ years
Note: "The Rule of 72" applies only when interest and dividends are reinvested, and it does not take taxes into consideration.

THE TEN DUMBEST MISTAKES
PEOPLE MAKE ABOUT MONEY

1. Being Ashamed to Invest Small Amounts. With this attitude, you'll never save anything. What is small to one investor may be huge to another. **Solution:** Begin saving something from your next income or salary check. The dollar amount is not important. Developing the habit of saving is. Then, read Appendix C, Nine Easy/Painless Ways to Save.

2. Having Inadequate Emergency Savings. Without this nest egg you could wind up deeply in debt. **Solution:** Stash three to six months' worth of living expenses in a money market fund or bank CD. (Read Chapters 5 and 7.)

3. Leaving Cash in a Bank Savings Account. The interest rate is far too low. **Solution:** Move it immediately to a money market fund or money market deposit account. (Read Chapters 5 and 6.)

4. Operating Too Many Accounts. If you have several bank accounts, a number of mutual funds, and brokerage accounts, you're spending too much on service fees. And it's way too difficult to keep track of rates, prices, and other details. **Solution:** Consolidate. Have one checking account, one or two mutual funds, and one brokerage account.

5. Confusing Income with Appreciation. If you don't know what an investment is for, you're likely to hold or sell the wrong thing. Do not expect growth stocks and growth mutual funds to pay high dividends or income. Do not expect CDs, bonds, or utility stocks to rise in price. **Solution:** Read Chapters 13 and 17.

6. Avoiding Financial Goal Setting. Yogi Berra said it best: "If you don't know where you're going, you're probably going to wind up someplace else." Most people devote more time planning their vacations than their financial future. Consequently, they spend as much or more on cruises, airline tickets, and hotels than they do funding their retirement accounts or building up a nest egg.

Solution: Set just one or two specific goals. Write them down or discuss them with a stockbroker or financial adviser. Ideally, do both.

7. Failing to Diversify. It's tempting to put all your money in one place because it's convenient and easy. No investment is ever sufficiently profitable or safe to justify this lazy approach. **Solution:** Divide your assets among CDs, money market funds, stocks, bonds, Treasuries, and real estate.

8. Procrastinating. Most of us put off making financial decisions because we're afraid we'll do the wrong thing. **Solution:** Set time deadlines and take several small, easy investment steps, one at a time. For example, if you have $3,000 on hand in week number one, put one-third into a money market fund. The next week, buy a bank CD. The following week, use the remaining amount to buy shares of a blue chip mutual fund.

9. Ignoring Savings Plans at Work. Tax-deferred 401(k) or stock purchase plans are good deals, especially if your company matches your contribution. So are automatic EE Savings Bond programs. **Solution:** Talk to your benefits officer this Monday, and read Appendix C, Nine Easy Painless Ways to Save.

10. Failing to Have a Will. If you care about other people, keep an updated will. **Solution:** Call your lawyer this week.

PART ONE

Safe Stashing for Your First $50

1

Institutional Cookie Jars: Banks

"That's where the money is," Willie Sutton told a reporter when asked why he robbed banks.

Some of your money should be in one, too. And for that first $50, a bank savings account is the most logical place to begin.

Selecting a Bank

Like Willie, you want the best bank possible for your $50. However, not all banks treat all customers equally. So don't make a mad dash to the bank on the corner. It pays to shop around, even with only $50 burning a hole in your pocket. Eventually you will become a larger depositor and will need to use the bank for other reasons—a loan, a mortgage, or a checking account and other services you may want later on.

3

BANK SAVINGS ACCOUNT

For Whom

- Small savers
- Those with less than $500

Where to Open

- Banks
- Savings and loan association

Fees and Minimum Balance

- No opening fee
- Monthly fees vary if balance drops below certain level

Safety Factor

- High
- Deposits insured up to $100,000 at all FDIC (Federal Deposit Insurance Corporation) insured institutions

Advantages

- Safety
- Geographically accessible
- Withdrawal upon demand, aka "liquidity"
- Principal is guaranteed up to $100,000 by federally backed insurance corporation if bank is FDIC insured
- When account is sizable, it can often be used as collateral for a loan

Disadvantages

- Interest rate is low and fixed
- Checks cannot be written against the account
- Monthly fees on low balances may mean you will lose money

Since most Americans are always in a hurry, the single most common factor in deciding where to bank is, of course, location. Yet your nearest bank is not necessarily the right choice.

Before opening a savings account, check out your neighborhood bank, by all means, but also make personal visits to several others. At each one make an appointment with the person in charge of new accounts. Describe your financial needs; pay attention to what this person suggests. Don't worry about the quality of the wall-to-wall carpeting or the abundance of fresh flowers. Decor is not the issue, but other things certainly are.

Check to see:

- What the minimum deposit requirement is for a savings account.
- If all types of services are offered.
- How well rush-hour traffic is handled.
- If there are express lines.
- If there are branches near both where you live and where you work.
- If there are bank officers available to answer questions, or if you are likely to be sent scurrying from one desk to another, in a Kafkalike circle.
- If there is written material available on interest rates and service charges—material that you can actually understand.
- Then, compare fees and interest rates of all the banks you visit.

And check out **credit unions.**

Credit unions emerged in this country in the early 1900s to help those working class people who didn't qualify for loans from commercial banks. The members of a credit union pooled their money and made low-interest loans to one another. Today credit unions serve groups of people with a common bond (see Chapter 2 for more on these institutions).

Although banks are free to pay whatever rate they choose, as of late 1996 they were paying 1.8 to 2.9 percent on savings accounts while credit unions were averaging 3.3 percent. That should tell you something.

The stated rate, however, is only the tip of the iceberg. It is also important to know exactly how often the interest will be paid, because every time your account is credited with interest, you'll earn interest on that interest, which is known as **compounding**.

5

So open your account at a bank where interest is compounded daily, not quarterly. You'll make more money.

Passbook and Statement Accounts

If you have a small amount to invest, you'll obviously need to begin with a bank that will be happy to take your deposit. In a small-town bank it may be only $50, while a larger bank may require $300 or more.

Historically, banks offered two types of savings accounts: **passbook accounts** and monthly **statement accounts.** Although most have done away with the passbook type, there are still a few around. Savers receive a thin booklet in which the bank records all deposits, withdrawals, and interest payments after each transaction. You take the book to the bank each time you put in or take out money.

With a statement account, on the other hand, you do not have a booklet. Instead you receive a printed monthly statement detailing all transactions. Its advantage: You do not have to worry about losing your passbook.

Most banks have either a passbook or a statement type account and don't give you a choice. Some, however, have both, paying slightly different interest rates on each. If the bank offers both, ask what the rates are on each.

Fees

In many banks, if your balance falls below a certain amount, you will be assessed a monthly charge or you will lose interest, or possibly both.

Or, if your account is inactive, meaning you have not made a deposit or withdrawal during a certain time period, banks typically charge a small monthly fee.

Yield

Banks often advertise two figures: the annual interest rate and the **effective yield**. The difference between the two depends on how often interest is credited to your balance, thus increasing the principal on which interest is paid. A 3 percent interest rate has an effective annual yield of 3 percent if the interest is credited annually. If it is credited quarterly, the effective yield is 3.094 percent, and if interest is credited monthly, the effective yield is 3.116 percent.

Coupon Clubs

It's certainly gimmicky, but if it helps you save, then give the bank coupon club a try.

The coupon club is the generic name for a myriad of programs devised by banks to attract business. These include Christmas clubs, Hanukkah clubs, vacation clubs, and so forth. They are also offered by many savings and loan associations and credit unions.

If you decide to join one, each week or month, depending upon the club, you make a specified deposit or payment, enclosing a coupon with your money. At the end of a stated period, usually a year, your coupons will all be gone and your account full of money. In some clubs you cannot withdraw your money until the stated period is over. Ask.

COUPON CLUBS

For Whom

- Undisciplined savers
- People with large families who have to buy lots of holiday gifts
- Those who like tearing along perforated lines

Fee

- Usually none

Safety

- High

Advantages

- Forced way to save

Disadvantages

- Some clubs pay low interest or no interest at all
- Some pay interest only if you complete the full term of the club
- You may not be able to withdraw your money until the full term is over

---

Couponless Plans

In some banks, you can sign up for automatic savings deposit plans. You then designate the monthly amount you want to save, say $35. This amount is then automatically taken out of your checking account and deposited into your savings account, where it will earn interest. The record of your transaction is then attached to your monthly checking account statement.

$50 COMPOUNDED AT 5 PERCENT				
Compounding Periods Per Year				
Years **Annually**	**Semiannually**	**Quarterly**	**Monthly**	**Daily**
1 $52.50	$52.53	$52.55	$52.56	$52.58
2 63.81	64.00	64.10	64.17	64.20
10 81.44	81.93	82.18	82.35	83.43
20 132.66	134.25	135.07	135.63	135.90

(Source: Credit Union National Association, Inc.)

ATMs

Automated teller machines, electronic machines located on just about every corner of America, provide instant access to money 24 hours a day. To use an ATM you need an encoded plastic card issued by the bank, which is inserted into the machine, and a personal identification number (PIN). This PIN number is then punched in on the machine to access your account. Obviously you should never give your PIN number to another person nor have it written down in your wallet; instead pick a number that you can memorize, such as your wedding anniversary or your mother's birthday.

🛑 *Caution:* Don't pick your own birthday—thieves are on to that one.

Although ATMs are a godsend on weekends and when bank lines are long, use them with discretion:

- Check to see whether your bank charges for ATM transactions when you use its own ATM; if so, pick a different bank.
- Very often cards issued by one bank may be used in the ATM of another bank, but for a fee. Find out.
- Use a bank that is part of an ATM network, such as PLUS, MAC, MOST, NYCE, SAM, STAR, or Cirrus, in which case you can use your ATM when you're out of state or even overseas.
- Visa, MasterCard, and American Express can be used in many ATMs for cash advances. Check the fee for doing so.
- 🛑 *Caution:* On credit card advances you often pay service charges as well as interest beginning from the minute you receive the cash.
- Time your withdrawals. If you want money from your bank's money market deposit account where it's earning interest, make your withdrawal by ATM after 3 P.M., the bank's official closing hour. That way you'll get the maximum interest.
- ➤ **Hint:** Each bank sets a limit on how much cash you can withdraw on any one day. If you're planning to get cash for a trip, check the daily limit first.

Ways to Get the Most out of Your Bank

New electronic systems, revised banking rules, and expanded marketing programs all mean better deals for savvy bank customers. Read the examples below and then talk to your banker. These and other "deals" are not always advertised.

- *Currency exchange.* When abroad, get an exchange rate bargain by using a bank's automated teller machine (ATM) card to purchase foreign currency. Your PLUS or CIRRUS card, issued by U.S. banks that are members of one of these ATM networks, may be used at thousands of outlets around the world to withdraw local currency. The machine dispenses currency at an exchange rate that's several percentage points less than the official retail rate. And you don't pay the added transaction cost that many banks, hotels, and others charge for accepting U.S. dollar traveler's checks.

- *Buyer protection plan.* Goods purchased by using some bank-sponsored credit cards will double the standard one-year warranty for up to two years.
- *Senior citizens' programs.* Free checking, no-fee credit cards, free traveler's checks, and discounts on tickets to cultural events for its 50+ or 60+ customers.
- *Favorable loan and mortgage rates.* Banks often give preferential treatment to customers when it comes to lending money. Ask.
- *Fees waived.* Customers who combine deposits and loans and keep a minimum balance don't always have to pay service charges.

A Bank Checkup

- Ask your banker how interest is compounded.
- Get a printed chart of interest rates to study at home.
- Ask if the bank pays interest only on the lowest balance during the quarter. For example, if you have $200 in your account and you take out $75, then eventually build it back up to $200, is interest paid as though you had only $125 in the account all the time?
- Look for a bank paying interest from day of deposit to day of withdrawal.
- Will you be charged extra if you make many withdrawals?
- Are there any days at the end of the quarter when interest is not paid?
- How many days are counted in the bank's year? (Some banks have "dead days" at the end of a quarter when they don't pay interest.)
- If you take out money, or close the account at midquarter, will you lose interest?
- Are there penalties for leaving your account inactive for a long period?
- Is there a monthly service charge?

Study the chart on annually compounded interest in a $50 account and use it as a guideline for making your banking decision.

How Safe Is Your Bank?

Although occasionally banks fail, there's no need to tuck your money under the mattress. But you should:

- Bank only at federally insured institutions. Look for the FDIC sign at the bank. It stands for Federal Deposit Insurance Corporation, an independent agency of the U.S. Government that was established by Congress in 1933 to insure bank deposits. Member banks pay for the cost of insurance through semiannual assessments.
- Keep in mind that individual depositors, not accounts, are insured—up to $100,000, including interest and principal. That means if you have two accounts in the same name in one bank, you are insured only for $100,000, not $200,000.
- Find out how safe your bank really is. For a $10 fee, Veribanc, Inc., will send you a financial evaluation of any bank or savings and loan as well as its FDIC category—well capitalized, adequately capitalized, or undercapitalized. Contact: Veribanc, Inc., P.O. Box 461, Wakefield, MA 01880; 800-442-2657; 617-245-8370.
- If you discover that your bank is a weakling, move your money to the strongest institution in your area. Veribanc will provide the names of such banks for a $38 fee.
- **Hint:** You may wish to wait until any certificates of deposit mature before transferring money so as not to lose out on any interest.
- For information on FDIC insurance, call the consumer hotline at 800-934-3342, or write for a free copy of *Your Insured Deposit* to:
  Office of Consumer Affairs
  FDIC
  550 17th Street NW
  Washington, DC 20429

2

Credit Unions

Once thought of only as a place for assembly-line workers to get a car loan, credit unions are much sought after today by anyone who can become a member. They are an excellent choice for your first $50, and they inevitably pay one or two percentage points above bank rates. There is no lid on interest rates; they vary from union to union.

Credit unions are cooperatives, or not-for-profit associations of people who pool their savings and then lend money to one another. By law, they must have a so-called "common bond," which may consist in working for the same employer, belonging to the same church, club, or government agency, or even living in the same neighborhood. Because they are not-for-profits and because overhead costs are low, credit unions almost always give savers and borrowers better rates and terms than commercial institutions.

Theoretically, unions are run by the depositors—every member, in fact, must be a depositor, albeit a very small one. The true organizational work, however, is done by volunteer committees in the smaller unions and by paid employees in the larger ones.

CREDIT UNIONS

For Whom

- Members and members' families

Where to Find

- Your place of work
- Your neighborhood association
- Church, club, synagogue, YMCA, YWCA

Minimum

- You must buy at least one share to join a credit union
- Shares are determined by each union and vary from $5 to $30, with most around $15. (A share is really your first deposit.)

Safety

- Varies, but generally above average
- High if insured by National Credit Union Share Insurance Fund

Advantages

- Friendly, supportive attitude toward members
- Interest rates on savings are generally higher than at commercial institutions
- Interest rates on loans are generally lower than at commercial institutions
- Other services may be offered, such as mortgages, credit cards, checking accounts, IRAs, CDs
- An automatic payroll deduction savings plan is frequently available

Disadvantages

- Might be run by inexperienced volunteers or inadequately staffed
- Might not be adequately insured
- May not return canceled checks

➤ **Hint:** If you are not already a member of a credit union, but would like to be one, call the industry's trade organization for information on how to join or start a credit union:

Credit Union National Association 800-358-5710

Before you invest your $50 in a credit union:

- Make sure the credit union is insured by the National Credit Union Share Insurance Fund, a federal agency.
- Check it out by calling the agency at 703-518-6300.
- And inquire about its services from members.

3

Uncle Sam and Savings Bonds

The bank isn't the only safe place for your $50. Uncle Sam is willing and eager to keep it for you and, in return, provide a little something in the way of interest through what is known as a U.S. Savings Bond. (When you buy a U.S. Savings Bond you are lending money to the U.S. Government.)

Series EE Savings Bonds are an easy way to save small amounts of money (known as preserving capital) and at the same time earn interest.

You can buy EE bonds at most banks and there's no fee. The purchase price is actually 50 percent of the bond's face value, so in other words, a $50 bond costs only $25. (EE Savings Bonds are sold in the following face value amounts: $50, $75, $100, $200, $500, $1,000, $5,000, and $10,000.)

If you hold them until maturity, you'll get back the face value, $50 in the case of a $25 bond. In other words, both the principal (the $25 in this example) and interest are paid in a lump sum when the bond is redeemed at maturity.

Interest rates vary depending on when a bond is purchased and how long it is held. If bonds earn an average of 4 percent per year, the full face value will be reached in 18 years; at 6 percent, in 12 years.

One of the great plusses to EE bonds: The interest you earn is exempt from state and local income taxes and personal property taxes. You do, however, have to pay Federal income, gift, and estate taxes.

↗ **Hint:** There is, however, a way to avoid Federal income tax that is related to using the bonds for college tuition. See Appendix B, Seven Steps Toward College Tuition, for full details.

In addition, you have the option of not reporting the federal income tax until you redeem the bonds, or you can report the interest every year as it accrues. Check with your accountant.

EE Bonds issued on or after May 1, 1995 earn interest based on the yield on Treasury securities. Interest is added every six months to the redemption value of the bond rather than being paid out to you, the bondholder. There's a true benefit to not receiving interest payments until you redeem your bonds: You won't be able to spend the interest.

🛑 *Caution:* Bonds stop earning interest at final maturity date, and at that point, they should be redeemed then or rolled over into Series HH Bonds. And remember, you cannot cash in EEs during the first six months after you purchase them.

At Work

In addition to buying these bonds at the bank, you may also buy them through automatic payroll deduction plans—if your employer participates in this program. This is a great way to stockpile small dollar amounts, especially if you're not a natural saver. In fact, after a while you won't even miss the amount taken from your paycheck.

↗ **Hint:** For the current rate on bonds, telephone 800-US-BONDS. The rate changes each November 1 and May 1.

EE SAVINGS BONDS

For Whom

- Those who can wait several years for their return
- Those who have a low tolerance for risk and want to be certain that their principal is safe

Where to Purchase

- Banks
- Payroll savings plan
- Savings and loan associations
- Credit unions
- Federal Reserve Bank (see addresses on page 93)
- Bureau of the Public Debt, Securities Transaction Branch, Washington, DC 20239

Fee and Minimum

- No fee
- Minimum purchase, $25 for a $50 bond

Safety Rating

- Highest possible

Advantages

- Virtually no risk because the principal is backed by the U.S. government
- Interest is guaranteed
- Easy to buy at your local bank
- No commission or sales fee
- Income is exempt from state and local taxes
- Federal tax can be deferred until bonds are redeemed or mature
- EE bonds are an excellent way to save for a child's education, especially if you can target them to come due after he or she reaches age 14, at which point the interest income will be taxed at the child's lower rate. (Until the child turns 14, however, earned investment income from

assets in a child's name are taxed at the parent's presumably higher rate.)

- EE bonds purchased after January 1, 1990 by a bondholder at least age 24 and used to pay college tuition are free from federal income tax provided you fall within certain income guidelines when the bonds are redeemed. Ask your local bank for details.
- Upon maturity, you may reinvest—roll over—your Series EE Savings Bonds into Series HH bonds and further defer your taxes until the HH bonds mature, another ten years down the road. HH bonds can be purchased only by rolling over EE bonds that have reached maturity and are available in denominations of $500.

✚ Help!

- These publications are free from:
  Savings Bond Marketing Office
  Washington, DC 20226

  - *Investor Information Guide*
  - *Questions and Answers on the Education Bond Program*
  - *Guaranteed Minimum Rate Charts*

- For information on payroll savings and other details, call:
  Savings Bond Program
  202-377-7715
- Get these free IRS Publications by calling 800-829-3676:

  - *#550, Investment Income Expenses*
  - *#8815, Exclusion of Interest from Series EE U.S. Savings Bonds Issued After 1989*

PART TWO

The First $500

4
Interest-Paying Checking Accounts

It's a good idea to keep in mind that holding cash is actually an investment choice—there are a number of places where you can park $500 or more, earn interest, and have fairly easy access to your money. We will discuss the five best in the pages that follow. They are:

- Interest-paying checking accounts
- Money market mutual funds
- Insured bank money market deposit accounts
- Bank certificates of deposit (CDs)
- Treasury bills, notes, and bonds

Note: Savings accounts and EE Savings Bonds are two other choices, available for less than $500; they were described in Part One.

First, let's take a look at interest-paying checking accounts, sometimes called NOW accounts. NOW stands for Negotiable Order

INTEREST-PAYING CHECKING ACCOUNTS

For Whom

- Ideal for anyone who wants a checking account and can maintain the bank's minimum balance at all times

Minimum

- Varies from around $500 to $2,500 or more

Safety Factor

- FDIC-insured, up to $100,000

Advantages

- You earn interest on a checking account
- You can write checks for any dollar amount
- You may get overdraft privileges so checks don't bounce

Disadvantages

- Bank charges on regular checking accounts are almost universally lower than on these interest-paying accounts
- Minimums for maintaining accounts are steep

of Withdrawal. These are like regular checking accounts with printed checks and statements, but the good part is they also pay interest—anywhere from 1.25 percent to 2.5 percent.

Use them as a handy housekeeping account where you can earn a little interest on your cash balance as you pay your bills.

There's one real drawback attached to these NOW accounts: In order to earn the interest, you must maintain a minimum or a monthly average balance. Find out what it is. Minimums vary nationwide from about $500 to $2,500 or sometimes higher.

🛑 *Caution:* If you fall below the required minimum balance, you will lose interest and you may also be subject to per-check, per-deposit, and/or monthly charges.

The equivalent of this account at a credit union is called a share draft. Since credit unions don't have a cap on the amount of interest they can pay, share drafts generally offer slightly higher rates than bank accounts. (See Chapter 2 for more on credit unions.)

TIP: In today's competitive banking world, an interest-paying checking account is a good choice if you can maintain the minimum amount in order to avoid any steep fees and charges—these eat up any earned interest. Take time to do your calculations carefully. If you know it will be difficult for you to maintain the minimum balance, open a regular checking account instead.

5

Money Market Mutual Funds

After you've opened a checking account and accumulated an extra $500, your next step is to find a safe place to put your hard-earned savings. One of the best and safest choices is a money market mutual fund where you'll earn considerably more interest than in a regular savings or NOW account.

What Is a Mutual Fund?

To understand what a money market mutual fund is, you first need to know how mutual funds in general work.

A mutual fund is actually an investment company in which you (e.g., the public) buy shares. This means your investment dollars are pooled with those of hundreds of other investors and the combined total is invested by a professional manager in various things—stocks, bonds, Treasuries, CDs, etc.

The fund manager studies the market, interest rates, and other economic indicators, buying and selling those investments that best

THE TOP YIELDING MONEY MARKET FUNDS		
Fund	**Telephone**	**Minimum**
Dreyfus Basic	800-645-6561	$25,000
Fidelity Spartan	800-544-8888	20,000
Fidelity Cash Reserves	800-544-8888	2,500
Dreyfus Worldwide Dollar	800-645-6561	2,500
Strong Money Fund	800-368-1030	1,000
Alger Portfolio	800-992-3863	none

suit the fund's stated aim or goal. A fund's goal might be to achieve income, price appreciation, or tax-free returns for its shareholders.

The Powerful Advantages of Mutual Funds

The value of a fund is that one large pool of money can be far more effectively invested than hundreds or thousands of small sums. Each investor in a fund, no matter how large or small his or her investment, then owns a proportional share of what the fund owns, and receives a proportional return, without discrimination based on the number of shares he or she owns.

Types of Funds

There are many types of funds. Some are set up for long-term growth, some for immediate income, others for tax-free returns. Some take higher risks than others. Some are devoted exclusively to buying and selling stocks; others to bonds, and some, to a combination of the two.

What's in a Money Market Fund?

In the case of a money market fund, the goal is a high yield with minimum risk. Money market funds derive their name from the type of securities they invest in: "money market" securities.

Financial companies, large corporations, and the U.S. Government all borrow large sums of money for short periods of time by issuing

WHAT KINDS OF THINGS MONEY MARKET FUNDS BUY

Agency securities. Issued by government agencies such as the Government National Mortgage Association (Ginnie Mae) and the Small Business Administration or by government-sponsored organizations such as the Federal National Mortgage Association (Fannie Mae) and the Federal Home Loan Banks.

Bankers' acceptances. Commercial notes guaranteed by a bank.

Certificates of deposit. Large-denomination negotiable CDs sold by both U.S. and foreign commercial banks. When over $100,000, they are known as "jumbo CDs."

Treasury bills and notes. Sold on a periodic basis by the U.S. Treasury and backed by the "full faith and credit" of the government.

Repurchase agreements. "Repros" are buy-sell deals in which the mutual fund buys securities with an agreement that the seller will actually repurchase them within a short time—generally seven days or less—at a price that includes interest for that time. The fund holds the securities as collateral.

Yankee CDs. Certificates issued by U.S. branches of foreign banks.

(or selling) money market securities in exchange for cash. (Short periods of time means one year or less.)

For example, the government borrows by way of selling Treasury bills, notes, and bonds. Large corporations do so by issuing IOUs called commercial paper, and banks by way of large certificates of deposit, called jumbo CDs.

These money market securities make up the fund's portfolio, rather than stocks and bonds.

The borrowers—the government, large corporations, and banks—are all good credit risks. They consist of the country's most solid institutions and they all agree to pay back the money quickly and at high interest rates. That's why you can earn more in a money market fund than in a traditional savings account.

Obviously, no ordinary saver would be able to participate in this venture on his or her own. The amounts involved are simply too large. Yet through a money market mutual fund, you, the average investor, can indeed share in this opportunity, safely and cheaply. The money earned by the fund after expenses is in turn paid out to you, the shareholder, as interest or "dividends."

Picking the Best Money Market Fund

STEP #1

Although many funds require a minimum deposit of $1,000 or $2,000 just to open an account, there is one fund with no minimum opening requirements—and, it's a good place to begin. Call and get a copy of the prospectus and account application:

> Alger Money Market Portfolio
> 800-992-3863

With a money market fund, you have what's known as liquidity—you have immediate access to your money without any penalty. You can cash in your shares by phone, mail, or through your broker if you have a brokerage-sponsored fund. And funds will wire money directly into your local bank if you so arrange in advance.

You can also tap your money by writing checks against your shares. Usually a fund permits unlimited check writing just as long as the checks are for amounts over $500. And the nice thing about it is, the checks are free.

STEP #2

If you want a fund that will let you write checks for any amount, look into these two; they have an opening minimum of only $500:

- Money Market Management
- Liberty U.S. Government Money Market Fund

Both are part of the hugely successful mutual fund company Federated Investors in Pittsburgh, PA (800-245-2423).

If you have $500, here are two funds that will let you open a money market account with that amount. If they are paying a higher interest rate than the Alger Fund, you know what to do.

Franklin/Templeton Money Fund
800-237-0738

Oppenheimer Money Market Fund
800-525-9310

➤ **Hint:** Many money market funds, including the two mentioned above in Step 3, will waive their opening minimum if you sign up for their automatic savings plan. In some cases, there's no opening minimum. *Ask.* In this type of plan, you agree to invest a certain amount, usually $25, a month, which is taken automatically from your checking account and wired into your money market fund.

✚ **Help!** There are hundreds of these money market mutual funds open to individual savers. Begin by calling those listed in this section. If you want a complete directory, send $8.50 to:

The Investment Company Institute
1401 H Street NW
Washington, DC 20005
202-326-5800

The pamphlet contains the names, addresses, and toll-free telephone numbers, as well as the initial and subsequent investment minimums, of each fund.

Safety

How safe are money market funds? Although they are not federally insured, they are considered very, very safe. Since they were launched in the early seventies, only two out of hundreds have run into trouble. Back in 1979, First Multifund of New York, which was paying an extremely high rate—93 cents on the dollar—closed its doors. More recently, Community Bankers U.S. Government Money Market Fund was forced to liquidate due to risky derivative investments.

The reason money market funds are considered so safe is that regulations require that only 5 percent of a fund's assets may be held in obligations of any one institution other than obligations of the U.S. Government.

Hint: The safest funds of all, of course, are those that invest only in U.S. guaranteed securities. You will certainly sacrifice a point or two in exchange for safety, but do so if it means you'll sleep better. Among those to consider are:

> Capital Preservation Fund
> Twentieth Century/Benham Group
> 800-345-2021
>
> Fidelity U.S. Government Reserves
> Fidelity Investments
> 800-544-8888
>
> T. Rowe Price U.S. Treasury Money Market Fund
> T. Rowe Price
> 800-638-5660
>
> Vanguard Money Market Reserves Treasury Portfolio
> The Vanguard Group
> 800-662-7447

Tax-Exempt Money Funds

The dividends you earn on most funds are fully taxable. Yet there are some funds that invest solely in tax-exempt securities—and their dividends are not taxed by the IRS at the federal level, only at the state and local levels.

Caution: Unless you're in a high tax bracket, it doesn't pay to buy into a tax-exempt fund because their yields are considerably lower than those paid by taxable money market funds (see page 31).

Hint: However, for the day when your taxable income puts you in a high tax bracket, you will want to consider investing in a tax-free money market fund. Among the best:

Dreyfus Tax-Exempt Money Market Fund
800-645-6561

Franklin/Templeton Tax-Exempt Money Market Fund
800-237-0738

Lexington Tax-Free Money Fund
800-526-0056

Double and Triple Tax-Exempt Money Funds

If you live in a state with high income tax rates, you can get an even bigger tax break from a fund in which the interest earned is free of state and federal income taxes and, in many cases, from local taxes. A list regularly appears in the financial pages of major newspapers, in *The Wall Street Journal, Barron's,* and popular money magazines.

Among the states with particularly high taxes: New York, California, Minnesota, Michigan, Massachusetts, New Jersey, Pennsylvania, and probably yours!

Call these mutual fund companies and ask if they have such a fund for the state in which you live:

Calvert 800-368-2748

Dreyfus 800-645-6561

Fidelity 800-544-8888

Franklin 800-237-0738

Lexington 800-526-0056

T. Rowe Price 800-638-5660

Vanguard 800-662-7447

✚ **Help!** Two services provide continually updated professional rankings and safety ratings for money market mutual funds. Call or write for complimentary copies of these two newsletters:

SHOULD YOU BUY A TAX-EXEMPT FUND?

To determine if a tax-exempt fund is worthwhile:
1. Subtract your tax bracket (28 percent in this example), from the number 1.
   1 minus .28 = .72
2. Then, divide the tax-free yield the fund is paying by .72 to find the taxable equivalent.
3. The result is the yield you'd need on a taxable investment to match the tax-free yield. For example, if a tax-free investment is yielding 5.5 percent, divide 5.5 by .72. The result, 7.64, is the yield you'd need to beat with a taxable investment if you're in the 28 percent tax bracket.

Income Fund Outlook (monthly; $49/year)
Institute for Econometric Research
220 SW Tenth Street
Deerfield Beach, FL 33442
954-421-1000

The Money Letter (bimonthly; $88/year)
Agora Financial Publishing
1217 St. Paul Street
Baltimore, MD 21202
800-433-1528

6

Bank Money Market Deposit Accounts

Top-notch protection and liquidity. This almost unbeatable combination is available when you open a money market deposit account (MMDA) at your bank. These accounts are insured for up $100,000 and also pay money market rates. You can tap your money at any time without penalty as long as you maintain the minimum required deposit.

They are, in fact, an insured variation of the regular money market fund we just discussed in the last chapter.

The Rules and Regulations

These accounts are not very complicated, but there are a few points you should be aware of:

- Individual banks determine the minimum required.
- Penalties can be imposed if you fall below the minimum.

- You can write only three checks per month (to a third party) against your balance.
- You are allowed to withdraw money in person as often as you like, as long as you maintain the required minimum balance.
- Usually there is no minimum amount on the size of the checks you write.

Regarding Interest Rates

The interest rate on bank money market deposit accounts is generally, but not always, just half a percentage point below that of Treasury bills. Banks adjust the rate they pay periodically, along with changes in short-term interest rates.

However, their yields tend to be a little lower than for money market funds. For example, as of early 1997, the national average for bank money market deposit accounts was 2.68 percent, compared to 4.81 percent for money market funds.

A MUTUAL FUND OR A BANK FOR YOUR MONEY MARKET?

Money Market Mutual Fund	Bank Money Market Deposit Accounts
Best for those who switch from bonds to stocks to money market funds, as interest rates change	Best for those who want their savings federally insured
Best for those who plan to write checks against their account	Best for those who do not need to write more than three checks per month
You can write as many checks as you like, with $150 or $500 minimums per check common	You can write only three checks per month to third parties
No service charges	Penalties for dropping below the minimum balance
Not insured	Insured up to $100,000

Receiving Your Interest

There is an important difference in the way in which interest is paid to depositors of bank money market deposit accounts and to shareholders in a money market mutual fund.

- Money market mutual funds must pay out most of their earnings to the fund's shareholders. Only a small percentage is retained—to cover the cost of running the fund.
- Banks, on the other hand, are not required to pay out all that your account earns. They are obliged by law, however, to post each month the interest rate they are paying.
- Although banks can pay whatever rate they want, in general you can expect bank rates to be lower than those paid on money market funds, as noted above. The reason: The money in the bank is FDIC insured. Mutual funds do not carry insurance.

BANK MONEY MARKET DEPOSIT ACCOUNT

For Whom

- Investors who know they can maintain the minimum balance
- Those who want to earn interest and have instant access to their money
- Those seeking a safe parking place for their savings or their emergency nest egg

Minimum

- Determined by individual banks; typically: $1,000, $2,000, or $2,500

Safety Factor

- Very high
- Insured up to $100,000

Advantages

- Competitive interest rates

- You can transfer money to your checking account (three preauthorized transfers per month)
- You can withdraw money in person as often as you like
- You can take your money out easily and instantly if interest rates drop

Disadvantages

- Some banks impose penalties for withdrawal
- You must maintain a minimum balance
- You can write only three checks per month
- If your balance falls below the minimum, you may lose interest or be hit with a charge

Some Special Tips

- Find a bank money market deposit account that can be linked electronically to other accounts and to the bank's ATM. Then you can write more than the three minimum checks since there's no limit on how often you can personally make transfers.

    In other words, if the accounts are connected, you can keep most of your money in the higher-paying MMDA and transfer funds into your checking account only as you need to do so.
- Select a bank that allows you to connect your MMDA to a brokerage account so you can buy stocks, bonds, and Treasuries by phone.
- Look at the effective annual yield when comparing banks. It is easier to compare this figure than to try to decipher each bank's individual compounding methods.
- Find out if your interest rate will be lowered to the passbook rate if your account falls below the minimum.
- Use a bank that cuts the rate only for the days when your balance is below the minimum, not one that penalizes you for the entire week or month.

7

Certificates of Deposit

Certificates of deposit, called CDs, are time certificates sold by banks. They are issued for a specific dollar amount for a specific length of time.

If you are looking for safety and fairly competitive yields, this is the place for you. All you need to do is agree to leave a certain amount of money with the bank or credit union for the stated time period—anywhere from a few months to several years. When that time period is up, your CD "matures" or "comes due" and you get the full amount back, plus interest.

CDs purchased at FDIC-insured institutions are insured for up to $100,000. Minimum deposits vary from several hundred dollars to several thousand. Huge CDs—those of $100,000 and up—are called jumbo CDs. They tend to pay higher rates than lower-denomination CDs.

CDs with Unique Twists

Banks offer a number of variations on the traditional CD. Ask around. You may encounter one of these or something equally appealing:

- *Bump-up CDs.* Great if interest rates are moving up. You can move to a higher interest rate, usually once, during the term of the deposit.
- *Built-in CDs.* These carry built-in rate increases.
- *Penalty-free CDs.* Rather rare, but nice. You can withdraw a portion of your money without a penalty within a certain time frame.

What a Difference a Bank Makes

Because banks have various types of CDs, it is absolutely essential that you shop around. Don't assume that all institutions have more or less the same rates because it's just not true.

The national average for six-month CDs, as of October 1996, was 4.79 percent, yet CDs were available for as high as 5.9 percent.

CDS VERSUS OTHER CASH ALTERNATIVES

Versus Money Market Accounts and Funds

Although CDs of one year or less tend to pay slightly higher rates than bank money market accounts, you give up immediate, penalty-free access to your money.

Versus Treasury Notes

Before you buy a longer-term CD, compare its rate with that of a Treasury note (see Chapter 15). An advantage that T-notes offer is that their interest is free from state and local taxes. This is not true for CDs—their interest is fully taxed.

Minimums also vary. Rates vary. Compounding methods vary. Maturities vary. Penalties for cashing in early vary. Yes, in general, you will find that:

- Interest rates on similar CDs offered by different banks in the same city can vary by as much as 1 percent or more.
- You will earn more on your CD if the interest is compounded daily.
- Some banks "tier" their interest rates, which means they pay higher interest on larger deposits.
- Banks can set any maturities they wish.

CD CHECKLIST

- Call two or three banks as well as your broker or a discount broker to see who has the highest rate.
- Ask how the interest is calculated. Remember, daily is far better than weekly or quarterly.
- Review rates. You may get a slightly higher rate from a broker because the firm buys huge certificates of $100,000 or more and then sells them to the public in $1,000, $5,000, or $10,000 chunks. You may also get a higher rate because brokerage firms shop the nations' banks, seeking the highest yielding CDs.
- Know how your interest will be handled. Have it reinvested so you won't spend it.
- Find out the rating (that is, the financial standing) of the bank issuing the CD—if you're buying it from a broker. Merrill Lynch, for example, provides credit ratings on all its CDs.

Some banks will let you set your own maturity date in what are called "designer CDs." If you have to prepare for college tuition, for instance, you can buy a CD that comes due when your child goes off to school in September. Designer CDs are also ideal for anyone expecting a baby or retiring at a certain date.

➤ **Hint:** Watch for periodical local interest-rate wars and take advantage of temporarily higher rates and favorable terms during this time period.

Buying a CD from Your Broker

In addition to being able to buy CDs at your bank, you can also buy them through a stockbroker. The advantage: You escape those hefty early-withdrawal penalties that the banks impose. Why is this? You can sell your bank CD back to the brokerage firm you purchased it from before it matures.

Note: CDs sold by brokers pay the same rates as the banks that issued them and they are FDIC insured.

How It Works

First, you tell your broker what CD maturity you want. He will quote a rate. Since the bank pays the broker to sell its CDs, you will not be stuck paying your broker a commission. Then, you proceed to buy the CD.

Second, if you want to redeem your CD before maturity, you can sell it back to the broker without a penalty. Your broker can readily sell it to someone else in what is called the "secondary market."

🛑 *Caution:* The price of the CD will fluctuate depending upon what it's worth on the open market. In other words, your CD will go up in price if interest rates go down—that's because it is more prized by investors than newly issued CDs that are paying lower rates. That means it is possible to make a profit by actually cashing in a CD before its maturity date. On the other hand, your CD will decrease in value if money market rates rise.

Choosing a CD Interest Rate

Advertising by financial institutions may herald high rates in order to entice you and your money. But before you buy a CD from a bank, read the fine print and figure out the true interest rate. Here's what you need to look for:

- *Compounding.* Note whether the ad indicates whether interest is compounded or simple. Compounded is better because it means your interest earns interest. On a one-year CD that pays 5 percent simple, your interest rate is just that—5 percent. But when it's compounded daily, that 5 percent yields the equivalent of 5.33 percent over the course of a year.
- *Floating Rates.* Some CDs have floating rates in which interest is tied to an index, such as the rates paid on U.S. Treasuries. Banks should explain just what this means to you—they can tell you the initial rate, but of course, no one can predict precisely future rates.
- *Teaser Rates.* Some CDs offer a really high introductory rate, which then, of course, drops. The high rate is apt to appear in the ad in bold face whereas the lower rate will be in the fine print. Ask how long the high rate will be in effect.
- *Rollover Rates.* Find out if you will be notified when your CD is coming due; if you are not and you forget, will it be rolled over into another CD? If so, the new CD might be paying a lower rate—something you certainly want to avoid.

➤ **Hint:** Check the Wednesday edition of *The Wall Street Journal*, the Friday edition of *USA Today,* or your Sunday newspaper for a listing of the nation's highest-yielding CDs. If rates are significantly higher out of town, call for instructions for purchasing them. Make certain any CD you buy is FDIC-insured.

8

Mini-Investor Programs

Once you have tucked away a small nest egg, believe it or not, $500 can move you into the stock market. There are several interesting programs designed for the mini-investor, but remember, stocks are much riskier than any of the previously discussed investments.

🛑 *Caution:* These mini-programs are *not* designed to replace your savings. They are merely an inexpensive way to buy stocks—they sidestep using a stockbroker and/or offer reduced commissions. Please do not participate until you have saved at least three months' worth of living expenses in your money market account or in several CDs.

What Exactly Is a Stock?

Before becoming involved in the stock market, it's only logical that you understand what a stock is.

A stock represents part ownership in a company, and anyone

who owns a stock is called a stockholder or shareholder. When a company wants to raise capital (usually to expand), it can do several things: It can borrow the money from the bank, it can issue (or sell) stocks to the public, or it can sell bonds. (Stocks and bonds are discussed in greater detail in Chapters 16 and 17.)

In order to document the fact that someone has purchased a stock, the company issues stock certificates to shareholders. This piece of paper shows the number of shares purchased at any one time by that person. If you buy more shares subsequently, you'll be given yet another stock certificate.

Making Money In Stocks

If the company is profitable, you, as a shareholder, can make money in two ways: through dividends and/or appreciation. A **dividend** is a periodic payment (almost always a cash payment) made from a company's earnings to stockholders. Most dividends are paid out four times a year. The board of directors can increase, decrease, or even cancel dividends, depending upon the company's profits.

Dividend payments vary from company to company. In fact, some never pay dividends. Those that consistently do are known as income stocks and investors buy them precisely because they want the steady cash payments. Utility stocks, discussed in Chapter 12, are known as income stocks.

The stocks of companies that pay no dividends, or very small ones, are known as **growth stocks.** Profits are reinvested in the company rather than used to make dividend payments. Investors buy them because they expect the price of the stock to grow over time. Growth stocks are riskier than income stocks, but they offer greater money-making potential; they are discussed in Chapter 17.

Buying Stocks

You may buy stocks in any publicly held corporation—one whose shares are traded publicly. (Some companies are privately held and do not sell shares to the public.) In addition to individuals, institutions also buy stocks. **Institutional investors** include mutual funds and employee pension funds.

Stocks are sold to the public in two steps: initially in the **pri-**

mary market, and thereafter these same stocks are resold to other investors through a stock exchange in what is called the **secondary market**.

The secondary market is not any one place but includes the New York, American, and regional stock exchanges as well as the over-the-counter or NASDAQ market. The exchanges are actually market-places where certain qualified stocks, approved by the exchange, may list their shares for buying and selling, known as trading.

Note: Although the price of a stock is fixed when it is initially offered to the public, its price thereafter continually fluctuates.

Here are ways you can get into the action with your $500.

Buying Stock Directly

You can bypass stockbrokers altogether by going directly to the company to purchase its stock. A growing number of public companies offer this service. Here are some examples:

Amoco
Bob Evans
Exxon
Houston Industries
McDonald's
Mobil
Reader's Digest
Texaco

The following companies allow first-time purchases for residents of the state in which the company operates:

Central Maine Power
Duke Power
Florida Progress
Green Mountain Power
Northern States Power
NUI
Puget Sound P&L
WICOR

You can purchase stock directly from these public utility companies—if you're a customer:

> American Water Works
> Boston Edison
> Brooklyn Union Gas
> Connecticut Energy
> Dominion Resources
> Minnesota P & L
> Nevada Power
> New Jersey Resources
> Union Electric

Hint: To find out if you can purchase stock from any publicly traded company without using a broker, write or call the Shareholder Relations Department.

SELECTED STOCKS WITH REINVESTMENT PLANS

Plans with No Discount	**Plans with a Discount**
Aetna	Bank of Boston
American Greetings	Citicorp
American Home Products	Citizens & Southwest
Bank of New York	Fleet/Norstar
British Airways	MNC Financial
Corning	J.P. Morgan
Exxon	Reader's Digest
Ford	Security Pacific
Harley-Davidson	Signet Banking
Hershey Foods	Southeast Banking
IBM	Time Warner
Kellogg	United Cities' Gas
Kimberly-Clark	USX
Merck	Wells Fargo
PEP Boys	
Schwab	
Tyson Foods	
Wisconsin Energy	

Dividend Reinvestment Plans

It Pays to Be a DRIP

No one likes to pay brokerage commissions, even to a friendly broker. In fact, commissions prevent some small investors from buying stocks at all, which is a shame.

Here's yet another way around this dilemma: Over a thousand companies allow existing shareholders to participate in a DRIP (Dividend Reinvestment Program). Here's how they work. You must already own stock in a company. Then, you can buy additional shares by automatically reinvesting your dividends.

A number of blue chip companies, such as AT&T, Clorox, DuPont, Heinz, Texaco, Procter & Gamble, and Kellogg, that pay above-average dividends have DRIPs. Some charge a nominal fee, but none charge what a broker would.

Some also offer 3 to 5 percent off the market price of new shares for even greater savings. Many allow shareholders to make cash payments into the plan in order to accumulate more shares in their accounts. Dividend investment is done entirely through the company.

➤ **Hint:** If you already own stock in a company, call the Shareholder Relations Division and ask whether it has a DRIP and, if so, how many shares you need to enroll. With some, a single share is sufficient; others require 15, 50, or 100 shares.

➤ **Hint:** For a complete listing of companies with DRIPs, contact: Northstar Financial, 7412 Calumet Ave., Hammond, IN 46324; 219-931-6480; cost: $15.95 including shipping.

Two More Low-Cost Ways to Buy Stocks

- *Buying One Share.* Individual investors may join the National Association of Investment Clubs (NAIC). Under NAIC's Low-Cost Investment Plan, for a one-time charge of $7 per company, you can buy as few as one share of stock, directly from more than 150 major participating corporations.

DOLLAR COST AVERAGING

While no investment plan is 100 percent risk-free, dollar cost averaging, a technique offered by the Blueprint Program™, can help cushion you from stock market fluctuations.

With dollar cost averaging, you invest the same fixed dollar amount every month in the same stock—say $25, $50, or $100. That means you buy more shares when prices go down and fewer when prices go up. Over the long run, you get a lower average cost per unit for the investments you make.

Note: You can cancel this plan at any time. You can also use dollar cost averaging on your own or with mutual funds.

Among the companies are: Whirlpool, Kellogg, Mobil, PepsiCo, and Quaker Oats. Most do not charge a commission, although a few require a nominal fee ($1 to $3) for each transaction just to cover expenses. All have Dividend Reinvestment Programs.

- *Buying at Work.* An increasing number of companies offer plans through which employees can buy stock in the company they work for. These are called ESOPs, or Employee Stock Ownership Plans.

Check with your benefits officer to see if your employer offers this option. However, never invest all your money in your own company—even the best have their ups and downs.

The Blueprint Program™

An inexpensive and convenient way for you to invest in stocks is offered by Merrill Lynch, the nation's largest full-service brokerage firm. Through its Blueprint Program™, you can invest any dollar amount you want, the initial minimum being $500.

The appealing part of this program is that you're investing by the

BLUEPRINT PROGRAM™

For Whom

- Any small investor interested in getting into the market

Where To Purchase

- Your local Merrill Lynch office, or from:
  The Blueprint Program
  Merrill Lynch, Pierce, Fenner & Smith
  PO Box 5380
  Denver, CO 80217
  800-637-3766

Minimum & Fees

- $500 initial minimum purchase
- Reduced commissions
- Transaction fee at $3.85

Safety Factor

- Like any stock, Blueprint holdings are subject to swings in the market

Advantages

- Low entry cost
- Reduced brokerage fees
- Automatic dividend reinvestment plan
- Toll-free telephone 24 hours a day for your account balance, securities quotes, trading
- Record keeping and tax data taken care of by Merrill Lynch
- Dollar cost averaging (see page 46)

Disadvantages

- You must pick your own stocks
- Stock market risk

dollar amount, not by the share, which means you can acquire fractions of shares as well as whole shares.

You may buy any stock that trades on the New York and American Exchanges and more than 1,000 over-the-counter stocks in which Merrill Lynch makes a market. Also available through the program: mutual funds managed by Merrill Lynch or its affiliates, and precious metals—gold, silver, and platinum.

Although you pay commissions, they are lower than the regular rate. There is also a processing fee charged for each transaction in your account—it's currently $3.85. Dividends are automatically reinvested. You'll receive a quarterly statement and a year-end consolidated tax-reporting statement.

The securities in the Blueprint Program™ are protected by the Securities Investor Protection Corp. (SIPC) up to $500,000, of which $100,000 may be paid to satisfy claims for cash.

9

Investment Clubs

Of all the options you have at your doorstep, a clubhouse will provide you with the most fun and enjoyment—if not the greatest return on your principal.

Joining an investment club is an excellent way to learn about the stock market, the movement of interest rates, and the overall economy. It's also a way to meet new people who, like you, are interested in learning how to turn a small amount of money into a sizable chunk.

Most clubs are small—the optimum size is about 20—and they meet once or twice a month in a community center or in a member's home. Members pool their money and jointly decide what stocks to purchase and when to sell.

Clubs require monthly payments that range from $20 per month to as high as the members dare go—several thousand dollars in some cases. Energetic hosts frequently combine the regular business meeting and discussion with coffee, dessert, or other refreshments.

How Clubs Work

The mechanics are simple. Making money, though, is not, especially if most members are inexperienced. Nevertheless, you will get your investment feet wet, and by combining your collective dollars and knowledge, you'll undoubtedly pick a winner or two, if not more!

If you don't know of a club in your area, ask at work or at your local YMCA or YWCA, adult education center, church, or synagogue.

Can't find one? Why not start your own with a few friends or colleagues. The eight steps are quite simple:

1. Find 12 to 20 people willing to join a club. Set the minimum investment requirement ahead of time—the average is $40 per month.
2. Select a person to be responsible for the paperwork. This task should rotate every few months.
3. Get details on how to get started from: The National Association of Investment Clubs, 711 West 13 Mile Road, Madison Heights, MI 48071; 810-583-6242. This is the umbrella group for all clubs. Your club may join NAIC for $35, plus $14 per member. You will then receive a stack of useful literature plus a subscription to *Better Investing* magazine.

   The NAIC also gives member clubs extremely useful and really solid advice on the legal aspects of organizing a club, conducting meetings, analyzing stocks, and setting up portfolios.

HOW MONTHLY SAVINGS ADD UP

Look at what happens if you invest $100, $300, or $500 each month at the fixed rate of 8 percent, not taking taxes into consideration.

Monthly Amount	5 Years	10 Years	20 Years
$100	$7,348	$18,295	$58,902
$300	22,043	54,884	176,706
$500	36,738	91,473	294,510

(Source: Credit Union National Association, Inc.)

For Whom

- Anyone

Minimum

- Set by individual clubs. Ranges from $20/month and up
- Members contribute a set dollar amount each month

Safety Factor

- Depends on the club's investment philosophy

Advantages

- Inexpensive and supportive way to learn about investing
- Reduces anxiety surrounding first-time investing and trading stocks
- Individual members of the NAIC can buy one share of any of a number of companies and thereafter invest small amounts periodically in these companies

Disadvantages

- You may earn a better return elsewhere, especially if your club is inexperienced or does not set sensible buy-and-sell guidelines
- Results are not guaranteed
- Investments are not insured
- There's a high mortality rate, with many clubs failing in the first 12 to 18 months

✚ **Help!** Read: *The Beardstown Ladies' Common-Sense Investment Guide* (New York: Hyperion, 1995; $19.95).

➔ **Hint:** Individuals can join NAIC for just $39. You should even if you're not a member of a club.

4. Establish firm guidelines regarding withdrawal of a member's funds and entry of new members.

5. Meet and invest on a regular basis—whether or not the market is doing well.
6. Reinvest all earnings in a diversified portfolio—one that has at least five different companies.
7. Use a discount broker to save on commissions.
8. Stick to regular stock buy-and-sell guidelines. All members should be responsible on a rotating basis for doing research and making recommendations to the club.

Do Clubs Really Make Money?

Yes, a great many of them do. According to a recent NAIC survey, in 26 out of the last 39 years clubs bettered the S&P 500's total return. The secret to their success: Member clubs consistently follow a planned program of patient, long-term investing. They adhere to these principles:

- Invest a fixed monthly amount, without regard to the stock market outlook. Clubs that try to outguess the market usually fail.
- Reinvest all earnings to benefit from compound income.
- Buy solid growth companies whose sales and earnings are increasing faster than the economy or faster than those of competing firms.
- Diversify investments to spread out the risk factor.

PART THREE

The First $1,000

10

Your IRA, Keogh, or SEP

Without a doubt, the very first $1,000 that you manage to accumulate above and beyond your emergency nest egg should be invested in a tax-advantaged retirement plan: an **IRA** (Individual Retirement Account), a **Keogh Plan,** a Simplified Employee Pension Plan, also known as a **SEP,** or a **401(k)** plan at work.

In all of these, the money you invest grows free of taxes until you take it out. That means interest and dividend income accumulates on a tax-deferred basis.

We'll look at IRAs, Keoghs, and SEPs in this chapter and at 401(k)s in the next. (A 401(k) plan is one in which your company deducts a certain amount from your salary upon your request and puts it into a retirement account. It is also known as a salary-reduction plan.)

Why You Must Have a Retirement Plan

Life expectancy for an American baby born today is about 73½ years. That means most of us will probably spend about 20 years or so in retirement. It goes without saying that preparing for those years is an absolute necessity unless we want to face melted cheese and tuna casseroles for dinner day in and day out.

And don't count on Social Security or government-supported medical benefits—these programs are continually under attack and their future remains questionable. It's best to regard Social Security in particular only as a way to pay for a very small portion of your retirement needs. As it is, at most, Social Security benefits replace only 24 percent of salary for someone earning $60,000 upon retirement and 43 percent of salary for someone earning $24,090.

Companies have wised up, too, and are not always inclined to be any more generous than they have to be. Pension plans have been trending downward and benefits are generally being reduced.

All About IRAs

The most common type of retirement account and the one available to the greatest number of people is an IRA. Here's how it works:

- Anyone who is working can put up to 100 percent of the first $2,000 he or she earns annually into an IRA every year. If you earn less than $2,000 a year—let's say $1,275—you could contribute that entire amount. But even if you're a rock star making millions of dollars every year, $2,000 is still the maximum you can contribute annually.
- You can open an IRA at your bank, brokerage firm, with a mutual fund company, or with many insurance companies. The paperwork is simple and you actually have until April 15 to contribute money for the previous tax year.
- Although there is a maximum yearly contribution of $2,000, your IRA will increase in value just through the interest earned or the dividends paid out. These additional dollars stay in the account along with whatever you contribute, until you retire and begin withdrawing your money.
- If, like most retirees, you're in a lower tax bracket when you retire, there will be less of a tax bite when you do start tapping your account.

- Beginning in 1997 both husband and wife can contribute up to $2,000 each year (total $4,000) even if only one spouse earns compensation.
- If you are divorced and receive alimony, you can make an IRA contribution even if all your income is from alimony. That's because alimony is treated as earned income.
- Your contribution is tax deductible on your 1040 form, provided neither you nor your spouse is an active participant in an employer-sponsored retirement plan and you are younger than age 70½ at the end of the year.

AN IRA VERSUS A TAXABLE INVESTMENT

Years	IRA Account	Taxable Account
5	$11,924	$11,867
10	28,130	27,568
15	50,627	48,343
20	82,369	75,831

- Even if you or your spouse is an active participant in a plan, you may still be able to deduct IRA contributions on a sliding scale; check with your accountant. The deduction is eliminated when adjusted gross income reaches $50,000 for a married couple or $35,000 for an unmarried person.
- Even if you are not eligible for the $2,000 tax deduction, you should still have an IRA. It is an easy and excellent way to accumulate tax-deferred earnings for the day when you retire (see box on page 63).
- You may have use of your IRA dollars once a year for a 60-day period through a procedure called a rollover in which you actually take money out of one IRA account and put it into another one.

STOP *Caution:* Unless your assets are in another IRA within 60 days, you will have to pay both income tax and an added 10 percent penalty tax. Some people find a rollover useful if they need cash for less than 60 days—but never take this money out unless you're absolutely certain you will put it back within the 60 days.

Numbers Don't Lie

Some so-called financial experts say there's no point in having an IRA if it's not tax deductible—don't fall for it. Investment performance in an IRA far outstrips similar investments made in a taxable account. Just look at the table above—it shows the benefits of putting $2,000 a year in an IRA that compounds at 8 percent compared to putting the same amount in a taxable investment. It's immediately clear which approach is the winner.

> **TIP:** Maximize your savings by putting money into your IRA as early as possible in the tax year. If you contribute at the beginning of the year instead of waiting until April 15th of the following year, your money will be earning interest for $15\frac{1}{2}$ months—giving you a great head start.

Where to Invest Your IRA, Keogh, or SEP

Whether you're inclined to be conservative or speculative, there's an investment program that's just right for your IRA, Keogh, or SEP. Several "custodians" are officially approved as places to set up these accounts—banks, brokerage firms, and mutual funds are the most popular. Take a look at all three before opening your account, taking into consideration how much money you have, your enthusiasm for monitoring your account, and your appetite for risk.

You should also ask what the annual fee is—it's officially known as the custodial fee and generally runs somewhere between $20 and $50.

➤ **Hint:** Be sure to pay the annual custodial fee with a separate check for two reasons: 1) So it won't reduce your account, and 2) If you mail it by December 31, you can deduct it on your tax return if your miscellaneous expenses exceed 2 percent of your adjusted gross income.

Too Many Custodians Is Not a Good Thing

Although you can divide your IRA contributions into as many investment choices and custodians as you like (as long as you stay within the dollar limitations), be smart and limit your accounts to one or two, three at the maximum. It's much too difficult and time consuming to keep track of more.

The IRS lets you fund IRAs with stocks, bonds, mutual funds, government and agency issues, CDs, foreign securities, covered options, and financial and commodity futures. It does not, however,

---

SOME NO-LOAD FUNDS FOR YOUR IRA

- Calvert Social Investment Growth
- Dreyfus Large Company Value
- Dreyfus Third Century
- Fidelity Mid-Cap Stock Fund
- Fidelity Pacific Basin
- Heartland Value & Income
- Neuberger & Berman Partners
- Strong Growth Fund
- Vanguard Windsor II
- Wellesley Income Fund

---

allow investments bought on margin, insurance investments, and collectible objects, except U.S. and state gold and silver coins of one ounce or less.

Using a Bank

The safest and probably the most convenient choice for a small IRA is a bank **CD** or certificate of deposit that is insured up to $100,000. Most banks charge little or nothing to set up and maintain an IRA. Some, however, impose monthly maintenance charges. That means, as in every institutional transaction, you must read the fine print carefully. (Bank CDs are described in full in Chapter 7.)

STOP *Caution:* There's some risk involved in buying a long-term CD—one that matures or comes due in five years. That's because if interest rates go up during that five-year period, your money is tied up, unavailable for buying the newer, higher-yielding certificates. So, unless rates are high, buy a one- to two-year CD so you'll have money coming due, which you can then reinvest if rates climb.

Using a Mutual Fund

The inner workings of mutual funds are explained in great detail in Chapters 5 and 13. But as far as the pros and cons of using one for your IRA or Keogh plan are concerned, here is what you should know.

Just about all mutual funds—which are companies that pool money together from individuals in order to buy a wide variety of stocks, bonds, and Treasuries—offer IRAs. Even though you can find a mutual fund specializing in gold, commodities, or foreign stocks, your own good judgment should steer you in more sane directions. Remember—you're saving for the day when you no longer have a steady paycheck.

SUGGESTED STOCKS FOR YOUR IRA

These conservative stocks are suggested for long-term total return:

Abbott Laboratories	Mobil Corp.
Atlanta Gas Light	Pfizer, Inc.
Brooklyn Union Gas	Sara Lee
Hershey Foods	Schering-Plough
J.P. Morgan	Walgreen Co.
Kellogg	Wrigley

These six stocks are suggested for their above average dividend yields:

American Brands	Southern Co.
Exxon	Texas Utilities
Jostens	Texaco

COMPARE BROKERAGE COMMISSIONS

	100 shares @ $10	100 shares @ $15	100 shares @ $20
Quick & Reilly	$37.50	$77.75	$109.00
Fidelity	46.50	101.00	143.50
Charles Schwab	47.00	101.50	144.00
Smith Barney	50.00	212.19	433.77
Merrill Lynch	50.00	205.00	373.00

➴ **Hint:** Most mutual funds reduce their opening minimums for IRAs—so a fund that requires $2,500 to open may let you buy shares for as little as $500. *Ask.*

Be sure you select mutual funds that invest only in money market funds, high quality blue chip or growth stocks—those that are likely to appreciate in value and/or pay high dividends. Funds with top-rated bonds are also suitable for an IRA.

THE 10 PERCENT PENALTY

Beginning in 1997, tax laws have changed regarding early withdrawal (before age 59½) of an IRA. The 10 percent penalty will not apply if you tap into your account in these cases:

- To pay for deductible medical expenses (those that exceed 7.5 percent of adjusted gross income) *or*
- To purchase medical insurance if you've received unemployment compensation for at least 12 weeks.

🛑 *Caution:* Never put your IRA in a tax-exempt mutual fund or a tax-exempt anything. Tax-exempts have lower returns or yields than taxable ones and, since IRAs are already sheltered from taxes, you don't need that feature.

Using a Brokerage Firm

At some point down the road, when you feel confident about picking your own stocks and bonds (or you have found an excellent broker) and you have at least $5,000 in your IRA account, you may want to open a "self-directed" IRA at a brokerage firm. You can manage the money or your broker can advise you on what stocks and bonds to put in your IRA.

When your IRA is small, this type of account is not a good idea. You simply don't have enough money with which to diversify, to spread out over several different stocks and thus protect yourself in case one of the stocks you select falls in price.

In addition, the brokerage fees are high in relation to the size of your account. If eventually, however, you do decide to run your own IRA and you feel confident about picking your own stocks and bonds, use a discount broker instead of a full-service firm—you'll save on commissions. (See box for a comparison of commissions.)

Disadvantages of an IRA

Now that you know all the plusses about owning an IRA, you should be aware that there are some drawbacks:

- IRAs are not liquid. Although you can withdraw money before retirement, the penalties for doing so are stiff.
- Withdrawals made before age 59½ are subject to a 10 percent penalty unless they are used for qualified medical expenses (see above).
- Withdrawals over $150,000 in any year are considered excess distributions and subject to a 15 percent excise tax.
- IRAs may not be used as collateral.

✚ **Help!** One of the most helpful booklets on IRAs is free. Contact your nearest Internal Revenue Service for a copy of publication #590, *Individual Retirement Arrangements (IRAs)*, or call 800-829-3676.

ADVANTAGES OF AN IRA

- Every dollar you contribute can be written off your tax return, if you are not a part of a qualified pension fund or if your income is below $25,000 (single) or $40,000 (married).
- If you or your spouse participates in a qualified retirement plan, you may be able to deduct some or all of your contributions depending upon your adjusted gross income (AGI). If you are single, a head of household, or married filing separately and your AGI is $25,000 or less, you can fully deduct your contribution; if your AGI is above $25,000 but less than $35,000, you can deduct part of it. On joint returns the range is $40,000 to $50,000.
- Penalties discourage IRA withdrawals prior to retirement and thus encourage saving.
- Interest and dividends earned are tax-free until withdrawn.

Keoghs and SEPs

Keogh Plans

If you are self-employed, either part-time or full-time, you should take advantage of the tax benefits offered by a Keogh Plan. Anyone who earns income from his or her own business, profession, or skill is entitled to participate in a Keogh in addition to an IRA.

➤ **Hint:** Even if you have an IRA or a private pension plan set up in which to save salaried income, you may still have a Keogh in order to shelter that portion of your income that comes from being self-employed. Don't miss this opportunity.

As with an IRA, you have a number of custodian choices: banks, savings and loans, brokerage houses, mutual funds, and insurance companies. Your contributions are deductible from your federal income tax, and the interest in your account accumulates free of taxes. The same early withdrawal penalties that apply to an IRA apply to a Keogh.

Here's where the two plans differ: In a Keogh you may contribute up to 25 percent of what you earn through self-employment—before tax deductions—for a total of $30,000 annually. If you have high self-employed income, that's a much better deal than the $2,000 IRA maximum. On the other hand, if you're self-employed part time, the 25 percent ceiling may be rather low.

SEPs

When an employer, which can be you as the sole proprietor, establishes a SEP, the employee then simply opens a SEP IRA. (See choices for an IRA above.) In other words, a SEP is effectively an employer-sponsored IRA. Individual accounts are established for each employee with contributions limited to 13.043 percent of earnings or $30,000, whichever is less. Certain SEPs can include a salary-reduction feature as with a 401(k) plan.

STOP *Caution:* You may want to consult an accountant when setting up either a Keogh or SEP plan, as the rules can be quite complex. Once a professional has made the initial arrangements, you can then fund it each year on your own.

11

Your 401(k) Plan

"I've got all the money I'll ever need if I die by four o'clock."
—Henny Youngman

One relatively painless way to make certain you have money to get you past four o'clock as well as through retirement is the 401(k) plan. Offered by many employers to employees, this savings plan has become increasingly popular since it was authorized by Congress in the early 1980s. Not only does it provide employees with an automatic way to save for retirement, it both reduces and defers taxes.

With this type of retirement plan, also known as a **salary-reduction plan**, you contribute a certain amount of your annual salary to a special retirement account that has been set up by your employer with an authorized institution.

The contribution is deducted from your paycheck, so you don't even miss the money. The amount deducted is listed separately on your W-2 form, but is not included in the amount listed for "wages, tips, other compensation." In other words, your contributions are made with pretax dollars. This contribution reduces your reportable salary, which in turn reduces your federal income tax liability.

Many 401(k)s have an added plus: The employer also contributes, in some cases matching dollar for dollar or 50 cents for each dollar the employee pays in.

Most plans let employees decide where to invest their contributions. The typical choices are the company's stock, a stock mutual fund, a long-term bond fund, a money market fund, and a guaranteed investment contract (GIC). (GICs are fixed-income investments sponsored by insurance companies with payment of interest and return of principal guaranteed by the insurer but not by the federal government.)

Generally, you can move your money among the different investments at least once a year.

STOP *Caution:* Although taxes are postponed until you start receiving the money, there is a 10 percent penalty tax for withdrawing money before age 59½. (See page 61 for the recent change in tax law that allows for medical exceptions.) And you must start taking distributions by age 70½.

Each company has its own particular rules. Ask your benefits officer to explain yours and to give you a written copy of the plan's guidelines and options.

Hint: Even if you are eligible for a tax deduction on your IRA, contribute to a 401(k), too, if it's offered where you work. Why? The maximum you can put into an IRA is only $2,000 a year, whereas the ceiling on a 401(k) is much higher and indexed for inflation; the 1996 ceiling was $9,500.

Withdrawing and Borrowing Money

Withdrawing Money

Under certain circumstances, you may be able to withdraw funds before age 59½, but only if you're facing a financial hardship—for example, if you need to pay funeral or medical expenses for a member of the family or, in some cases, to pay for a principal residence or avoid eviction.

The regulations, however, are very stringent. To be eligible for a hardship withdrawal, you must prove that you can't meet your needs by borrowing from a bank or tapping other savings.

Borrowing Money

Most plans, but not all, let participants borrow money—up to half the amount but not more than $50,000. You pay interest on the loan to your own account, typically a percentage point less than what banks charge on secured personal loans. By law, 50 percent of your balance has to stay in the account as security for the loan. The loan must be repaid at least quarterly and fully within five years— unless the money goes toward purchase of a principal residence.

➤ **Hint:** The interest rate is often lower than what a bank will charge and, of course, your interest payments are made back into your own account and not to a bank—a real plus.

12

Utilities and Hometown Companies

What Is a Stock?

A stock, as you recall from Chapter 8, represents part ownership in a company, and anyone who owns a stock is called a stockholder or shareholder.

Public Utility Companies

Stocks of public utility companies have traditionally been sound, high-yielding investments and as such are considered safe enough for "widows and orphans." Because of their generally solid dividends and high safety ranking, you can invest at the $1,000 level, even though other individual common stocks are better purchased with investments of $5,000 or more, or through a mutual fund.

🛑 *Caution:* In general, of course, the greater the risk element in an investment, the more money you should have to cushion any losses.

Utilities are also appealing because of their dividend reinvestment plans (see Chapter 8). Some utilities even offer a discount when their shares are bought through these plans.

You should be aware, however, that the utility industry is being deregulated and therefore increasingly competitive. That means you should invest only in utilities with strong balance sheets and the capacity to expand, either domestically or internationally—or both.

Hometown Stocks

Another type of stock that beginners are often successful at picking out for their portfolios is those of local companies. If you work for a corporation whose stock is publicly traded, you're apt to be very much in the know about its financial condition, its management, its product or service, and its future.

The same is true for companies headquartered in your area. Folks who live near Ben & Jerry's, Boston Chicken, the Pep Boys, or Snapple, or who tasted Mrs. Field's cookies, all knew about these first-rate, popular products long before the general public.

If it plays in Peoria, it's likely to play on Wall Street.

SIX HIGH-YIELDING UTILITY STOCKS

• Central & Southwest	6.6 percent
• Baltimore Gas & Electric	6.2 percent
• Duke Power	6.0 percent
• Southern Company	5.6 percent
• Pacificorp	5.5 percent
• Texas Utilities	5.3 percent

Ranked **** by Standard & Poor's; yields as of early 1997

How to Find Bright Lights and Hometown Talent

Begin in your own backyard:

Step #1

Read your local paper to keep up to date on company news and developments.

Step #2

Visit the local company's headquarters; ask to take a tour or meet with an official; explain that you're seriously considering buying stock.

Step #3

Get a copy of the annual and quarterly report. You can do this in person, or in the case of your utility, by phone. Call the investor or public relations department.

Then, read through it in order to determine if:

- Earnings per share are rising
- Dividends are increasing
- Plant construction is completed
- The area's population is growing
- The company is facing any lawsuits
- It is facing deregulation
- It has plans to handle increased competition

Step #4

Track the company's stock price for several weeks by looking in the newspaper; be alert to trends up or down. Avoid buying shares at their 52-week high. (See pages 120–121 for how to read stock market tables.)

Step #5

Call a local stockbroker for an investment opinion and research report. You can do this whether or not you have an account.

Step #6

Compare the brokerage firm's report with that in *Value Line Investment Survey* or Standard & Poor's *Stock Reports*. These two key reference tools are available at most public libraries and brokerage offices.

Value Line ranks stocks for safety; stick with those with a #1 or #2 ranking.

STEP #7

Read any press coverage of the company's prospects or problems.

STEP #8

If you decide to buy shares, do so through a discount broker to save on commissions and sign up for the company's dividend reinvestment plan (DRIP) if it has one.

PART FOUR

The First $2,000

13

Mutual Funds for Stocks and Ginnie Maes

"Money won't buy happiness, but it will pay the salaries of a large research staff to study the problem."

—Billy Vaughan

Vaughan probably didn't have mutual funds in mind when he made his famous statement, but he might well have. A mutual fund is a company that has a lot of portfolio managers that make investments for others—for individuals and for institutions.

When you buy into a mutual fund you are actually purchasing shares of an investment trust or corporation. Your dollars are pooled with those of hundreds of other investors, and these combined moneys are then invested and managed by a staff of professionals, known as portfolio managers.

Fund portfolios are widely diversified—among stocks of different companies, bonds of different issuers, money market papers, and Treasuries of different maturities. All this diversification helps insulate you against wide fluctuations in the prices of individual stocks.

How Mutual Funds Work

Mutual funds are **open-ended**—that is, like stocks, shares are continually available and they can be bought or sold at any time.

The price of a fund's share is called its **net asset value**, and this price or NAV is determined at the end of each business day when the fund adds up the value of the securities held in its portfolio, subtracts expenses, and divides the total by the number of shares outstanding.

How You Make Money

Mutual funds make money for shareholders in three ways:

1. They pay shareholders dividends and interest earned from the stocks, bonds, Treasuries, and money market papers held in the portfolio.
2. They pay shareholders capital gains distributions—if a stock or bond is sold at a profit.
3. Their net asset value (or share price) may rise in value if the value of the securities held in the fund increases. When this happens your shares are worth more, and you'll make a profit should you decide to sell.

➤ **Hint:** You can have your earnings—dividends and capital gains distributions—either reinvested in additional shares of the fund or have the fund send you a check.

Picking a Mutual Fund

Before beginning your search for the right fund, you need to know the difference between load and no-load funds.

Load funds, sold by stockbrokers and mutual fund salespeople, are "loaded" with a sales charge or fee. Commissions for the purchase or sale of a fund typically range from about 4 percent to $8\frac{1}{2}$ percent of the total price.

Keep in mind that this means the value of the fund must escalate by that amount *before* you can break even.

Hint: Since studies show there is no overwhelming evidence that load funds outperform no-loads, you might as well find one without a load or commission and save the difference. However, some people like to buy load funds because they trust their broker's recommendations.

No-load funds have no sales commissions. You purchase shares directly from the fund itself, not through a stockbroker. You simply call the fund's toll-free number for the appropriate papers.

It is true, however, that some no-load funds have hidden fees (see box on page 78).

And now some basic advice about selecting a fund.

STEP #1

Clarify your goals. You need to figure out if you want a fund for income or for growth (also known as "appreciation"). Do you want a fund that consists primarily of stocks or bonds or some of each? Do you want a high-risk speculative fund or a more conservative one?

Each fund has a different investment objective, so it is essential that you understand these differences long before buying shares.

You'll find the fund's objectives spelled out at the beginning of the **prospectus**, which is the official description of the fund, required by the Securities and Exchange Commission to be given to potential shareholders. For example, a prospectus might read: "Our primary objective is safety of principal and long-term growth through the purchase of high-quality stocks in growth areas of the economy."

Caution: Even no-load funds can charge 12b-1 fees—up to 0.75 percent of a fund's average net assets per year. An additional 0.25 percent service fee may be paid to brokers in return for providing ongoing information to shareholders. Unlike other fund fees, this one continues on and on, for every year you own shares.

STEP # 2

Study the types of funds. Funds fall into several broad categories. Some emphasize growth—that is, price appreciation—others focus on income. Some provide tax-free returns; many are conservative, while others are highly speculative.

In picking a fund, be realistic about how much time you really will spend monitoring its performance. The more speculative its portfolio, the more you need to keep your eye on it in order to know when to buy more shares, or when to sell and get out.

MUTUAL FUND LOADS OR FEES

Many mutual funds have no loads (fees), some have low loads or fees, and others have outrageously high ones. Here are the key terms you need to know before investing in any mutual fund.

- **Front-End Load.** A sales commission charged when you purchase shares in a fund. These sales fees may be as high as 8.5 percent, but most are 4 to 5 percent. The load compensates brokers or salespeople who sell the funds. So if you put $1,000 in a fund with a 5 percent load, only $950 goes to work for you in the fund; the rest goes to the broker or salesperson.

- **Back-End Load.** A fee imposed when you sell your shares. A typical back-end load fund charges 6 percent if you redeem shares the first year, 5 percent the second, and so on until the charge disappears completely. If you're forced to sell your shares before the load disappears, it can be an expensive experience.

- **Redemption Fee.** Not to be confused with a back-end load, this fee is charged by some fund companies in order to discourage frequent trading. Generally, it's charged to those who sell within a year of investing in the fund.

- **12b-1 Fee.** Named after the section of law that authorized it, this fee forces shareholders to pay some of the fund's sales and advertising expenses. It can be as high as 1.25 percent of assets, or $1.25 for every $100 you invest.

The basic types of funds:

- *Aggressive or speculative funds.* These seek maximum profit, but at a fast rate, often achieved by taking greater risks than other types of funds by selling short or even by borrowing money for additional leverage. Also known as "maximum capital gains funds."

- *Industry or sector funds.* These specialize in one type of stock, such as energy or health care stocks, realty or public utilities, technology, etc.

- *Income funds.* These invest primarily in corporate bonds and are not concerned with growth or capital appreciation. Some invest in high-dividend stocks. For more on bond income funds, see pages 110–111.

- *Balanced funds.* These maintain portfolios that combine common and preferred stocks and bonds. Their aim is to conserve the investor's principal, to pay current income, and to have long-term growth. Their portfolios often consist of leading companies that pay high dividends.

- *Growth and income funds.* These invest in common stock of companies that have had increasing share value and a solid record of paying dividends.

- *Municipal bond funds.* These are designed for tax-exempt income.

- *U.S. Government income funds.* These invest in a variety of government securities: U.S. Treasury bonds, federally guaranteed mortgage-backed securities, and other government notes.

- *Index funds.* These contain a representative basket of stocks mirroring the index, such as the Standard & Poor's 500. They keep pace with the market.

- *Money market funds.* (See Chapter 5)

STEP #3

Study their performance record. Rating services will tell you whether a fund is making or losing money over various time periods. Many financial magazines and newspapers publish these results on a regular basis. Check for them in:

> *Barron's*
> *Kiplinger's Personal Finance Magazine*
> *Money*
> *USA Today*
> *Your Money*
> *Wall Street Journal*

Once you've identified a type of fund, or a specific fund, read its current analysis in *Morningstar Mutual Funds*. This research service covers 1,500 mutual funds and rates them on the basis of total return, volatility, and performance. It also gives some interesting insights about the fund's portfolio manager. Updated biweekly, you can read it at your library, broker's office, or subscribe:

> Morningstar
> 225 West Wacker Drive
> Chicago, IL 60606
> $425/year; 3 month trial: $55
> 800-735-0700

↗ **Hint:** Take advantage of all of the fund's toll-free numbers. They're not there just to make transferring from one fund to another or buying and selling shares easy. Trained service reps will answer your questions about a fund's portfolio holdings, its risk factor, its objectives, etc. He or she will also provide updated information on what stocks or bonds a fund owns, its current share price, yield, and total return figures for one, five, or more years.

When to Buy or Sell Fund Shares

Even after you've selected a fund, you may be nervous about how it will react to sudden changes in the economy, to interest rates, or to the stock market. One way to resolve this problem is to keep your money in a family of funds that offers more than one type of fund under the same corporate roof. Some of the well-known fund families are: T. Rowe Price, Vanguard, Strong, Fidelity, Dreyfus, Oppenheimer.

Most funds offer free switching from one fund to another—or if there's a charge, it's a nominal one. The fund prospectus or the service rep at the 800 number will tell you if you are limited to a certain number of switches per year.

How do you know when to switch? It requires time and study, but in general:

- When interest rates fall, keep your money in a stock fund
- When interest rates rise, switch to a money market fund or a Treasury fund
- When the price of the stocks in a fund starts to slide, switch some of your investment into a money market fund; park your money there until you have a sense of where the economy is headed
- When the economy is growing, switch to a stock growth fund
- When you move up into a higher tax bracket, move into a tax-free municipal bond fund

Hint: No one fund should be regarded as economically viable for all times. The market is cyclical, the economy is constantly changing, and tax rulings are periodically revised—so never make an investment and think that's it. You must track the performance of all investments, including mutual funds, on a regular basis.

Help! These two letters advise readers on how and when to move among the various mutual funds. Ask for a sample copy before subscribing.

Fabian Investment Resource ($119/year; monthly)
2100 Main Street
Huntington Beach, CA 92648
800-950-8765

The No-Load Fund Investor ($129/year; monthly)
PO Box 318
Irvington-on-Hudson, NY 10533
800-252-2042

INSOMNIAC TRADING

If you're up all night, you don't have to wait until 9 A.M. to buy or sell mutual fund shares. Discount broker Jack White & Co., through its Global Link Program, matches fund buyers and sellers 24 hours a day, seven days a week. The company charges $33 plus 3 cents per share for trades up to $2,000; over $2,000 it's $33 plus 2 cents per share. **INFO:** 800-233-3411.

🛑 *Caution:* Many banks now sell mutual funds. But you should realize that these funds are *not* federally insured. If you wish to purchase shares in one, you must go through the same research steps as you would for any fund: Find out its investment goals, its risk factor, and, most importantly, its performance record.

Stock Mutual Funds

Buying shares in a stock fund is a good alternative to trying to pick from among the thousands of publicly traded individual stocks. For the small investor, the new investor, and the very busy investor,

---

SIX GROWTH FUNDS

These tend to outperform most other types of stock funds over the long term. They are best for those willing to assume a moderate degree of risk and those who can hold their shares at least two years, preferably longer.

• Strong Growth Fund	800-368-1030
• Columbia Growth	800-547-1707
• Franklin Growth	800-342-5236
• Guardian Park Avenue	800-221-3253
• Lindner Fund	314-727-5305
• Stein Roe Young Investor	800-338-2550

---

mutual funds offer diversity, professional management, liquidity, relatively low cost, and income and/or price appreciation.

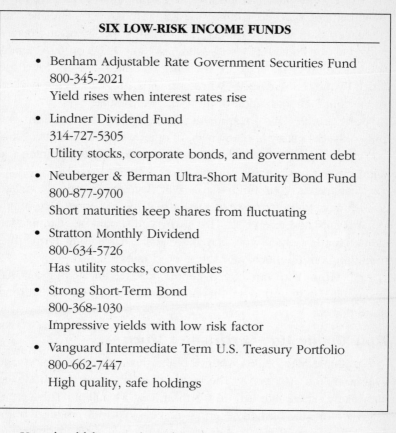

SIX LOW-RISK INCOME FUNDS

- Benham Adjustable Rate Government Securities Fund
  800-345-2021
  Yield rises when interest rates rise
- Lindner Dividend Fund
  314-727-5305
  Utility stocks, corporate bonds, and government debt
- Neuberger & Berman Ultra-Short Maturity Bond Fund
  800-877-9700
  Short maturities keep shares from fluctuating
- Stratton Monthly Dividend
  800-634-5726
  Has utility stocks, convertibles
- Strong Short-Term Bond
  800-368-1030
  Impressive yields with low risk factor
- Vanguard Intermediate Term U.S. Treasury Portfolio
  800-662-7447
  High quality, safe holdings

You should have at least $2,000 before participating in a stock fund, because there is a greater degree of risk here than in money market mutual funds, CDs, and savings bonds. Keep in mind that if the stock market falls, so will the value of a stock fund. On the other hand, if the market is bullish, stock funds will perform well. See the box for some suggestions.

Ginnie Mae Funds

These funds aim for high income and minimum risk and, more often than not, succeed. Ginnie Maes, short for Government National Mortgage Association (GNMA), are actually pools of mortgages backed by the Federal Housing Administration (FHA) or the Veterans Administration (VA). They are the only securities—except for those issued by the U.S. Treasury—whose principal and interest are backed by the "full faith and credit of the U.S. government."

(STOP) *Caution:* This government guarantee protects you from one thing only: default by homeowners. In other words, it guarantees that interest and principal will be paid—but it does not guarantee the value of your fund shares nor the interest rate.

That means your fund shares will fluctuate in price, for, like bond funds, when interest rates rise the value of Ginnie Mae mutual funds falls, and vice versa. That's why you should buy Ginnie Mae mutual funds only if you can hold your shares long term, thus smoothing out the fluctuations in interest rates.

➤ **Hint:** You can buy a Ginnie Mae certificate for $25,000 through a broker and avoid this problem of fluctuating mutual fund share prices.

How Ginnie Mae Certificates Work

A Ginnie Mae begins when a home buyer receives a mortgage insured by the FHA or VA. The lender then combines this mortgage with many others into a pool worth at least $1 million. This certificate—a mortgage-backed security—is then sold to a broker, who in turn sells pieces of it, also known as certificates, to individuals and to mutual funds. The "pieces" are typically sold in $25,000 units.

As homeowners make monthly mortgage payments, owners of certificates receive a share of the principal and interest payments on a monthly basis.

Although these are suitable for investors seeking a steady stream of income, *they have one problem:* When interest rates fall, homeowners rush to pay off their mortgages ahead of schedule and refinance at lower rates. When that happens, investors who own Ginnie Mae certificates receive their principal and interest payments sooner

GINNIE MAES

For Whom

- Investors who want a high yield

Where to Purchase

- Directly from a fund or through stockbrokers

Fee

- Load funds charge a sales fee (3 percent to 8.5 percent)
- No-load funds do not impose fees

Safety

- Relatively high, especially if held long term

Minimum

- $1,000 for funds; $25,000 for certificates

Advantages

- Yields tend to be slightly higher than Treasuries
- Provides monthly income
- You can reinvest income in additional fund shares

Disadvantages

- Fund yields are not guaranteed and could drop
- Some funds are allowed to sell options against their portfolios to keep the yields high; this adds to the risk level
- The price or net asset value of a fund's shares can drop

than planned. These investors then face the problem of reinvesting this money at the then prevailing rate, which of course, is lower than when they purchased their certificates.

How Ginnie Mae Funds Work

A fund operates quite differently from the certificates. You purchase shares of one of the funds. The fund manager buys and sells Ginnie Mae certificates in much the same way a bond fund manager trades bonds.

Therefore, with a fund, *your yield is not fixed*. The yield will rise and fall in relation to interest rates. And, of course, the fund's success also depends on the ability of the manager to buy and sell certificates at the most optimum time.

14

Socially Conscious Mutual Funds

Is it possible to be a successful investor and socially responsible at the same time?

Yes. "Socially conscious" or "green" funds are set up so investors can reconcile their desire for profits with their concern about environmental, political, and social issues. Unlike most mutual funds, which base their portfolios primarily on financial considerations, these funds apply other criteria, called "social screens" to the selection process.

Although each fund's screen differs, most refuse to invest in weapons manufacturers and utilities that rely on nuclear power. Some screen out the so-called "sin" stocks: tobacco, liquor, and gambling, as well as companies that are heavy polluters. Many avoid companies that use animals for testing or that lack a strong policy of hiring and promoting women, gays, and minorities.

Here are some picks in various categories:

Growth Stock Funds

These invest in stocks expected to provide long-term capital appreciation for shareholders. They have more volatile price swings than the more conservative income and balanced funds, described next.

- Dreyfus Third World Century 800-645-6561
- New Alternatives 516-423-7373
- Pioneer Capital Growth 800-225-6292
- Parnassus Fund 800-999-3505

Income Funds

- Calvert Social Investment Bond 800-368-2748
- Pioneer Bond Fund 800-225-6292

Balanced Funds

These funds seek the highest possible return consistent with a low-risk strategy. Their portfolios contain both stocks and bonds. They typically have higher dividend yields than growth funds and perform better when stocks are falling in price. In a rising market, however, they do not keep pace with growth funds.

- Pax World 800-767-1729
- Calvert Social Investment Managed Growth 800-368-2748

Money Market Funds

These funds do not invest in U.S. Treasury issues because, they maintain, those issues are used primarily to finance a federal deficit largely caused by heavy defense spending. Instead, these funds purchase issues of the Federal Farm Credit System, the Small Business Administration, and other government agencies.

- Working Assets/Citizens Trust 800-533-3863
- Calvert Money Fund 800-368-2748

✚ Help!

For more information:

Clean Yield Newsletter ($80/year; bimonthly)
Box 117
Greensboro, VT 05841
802-533-7178

Profiles two stocks per issue and updates eight others. Screens companies for their environmental practices and weapons production.

15

Treasuries for Ultrasafe Income

"Blessed are the young for they shall inherit the national debt."
—Herbert Hoover

When Hoover was our 31st president, he probably never dreamed that our national debt could reach $5 trillion. But it has, and to help finance it, the government issues Treasuries—Wall Street-ese for Treasury bills, notes, and bonds.

Regardless of your position on our country's debt, Treasuries are among the safest of all investment vehicles. You can get in on the action with $1,000, $5,000, or $10,000. They have four factors very much in their favor:

- They are the safest form of investment because the U.S. government guarantees to pay you back
- They are extremely liquid and can be sold at any time
- The interest earned is exempt from state and local taxes

90

- You can buy them through the Federal Reserve without paying a fee

What Are Treasuries?

Where do these Treasuries come from? Uncle Sam constantly borrows money, not only to finance building battleships but also to cover the federal deficit by issuing or selling short-term Treasury bills and longer-term notes and bonds to investors. (The difference among the three—bills, notes, and bonds—is the time limit or maturity. They run from a minimum of 13 weeks to a maximum of 30 years.)

- **Treasury bills** mature in a year or less. They come in 13-, 26-, and 52-week maturities and require a minimum investment of $10,000. Instead of paying interest, they are sold at a discount, that is, below face value.

  ↗ **Hint:** If you don't have $10,000 to buy a T-bill, consider a Treasury-only money market fund, such as Benham's Capital Preservation Fund, which has a minimum investment of $2,500. Call 800-345-2021 for a prospectus. This fund, which invests in Treasury bills and notes, provides income that is free from state and local but not federal taxes.

- **Treasury notes** mature in two to ten years and require a minimum investment of $5,000 for those maturing in less than four years, and $1,000 for those maturing in more than four years.

- **Treasury bonds** mature in 10 years or more, to a maximum currently of 30 years. The minimum investment is $1,000.

- **Inflation-indexed notes**. Offered for the first time in January 1997, these 10-year notes have a new twist: Both the bond's principal value and the amount of interest paid each year will increase along with the consumer price index.

Here's a hypothetical example from the *Wall Street Journal*:

- The interest rate is set at 3 percent
- Inflation runs at 2 percent
- Over the next 10 years, the bond's principal value will increase 2 percent annually
- As the principal increases, so does the dollar value of the interest paid
- With the interest set at 3 percent annually, each year the bondholder will get interest equal to 3 percent of the bond's continually growing principal value

---

U.S. TREASURIES

For Whom

- Investors seeking absolute safety
- Those with a minimum of $1,000
- Those who enjoy helping Uncle Sam

Fee

- No fee if purchased from Federal Reserve
- Flat fee from banks and brokerage firms

Safety Factor

- Highest possible
- Backed by the U.S. Government

Advantages

- Principal and interest guaranteed
- Maximum liquidity
- No state and local tax on interest earned

Disadvantages

- Awkward to purchase unless you use a stockbroker

THE TWELVE FEDERAL RESERVE BANKS

Atlanta

104 Marietta Street NW
Atlanta, GA 30303
404-521-8653

Boston

600 Atlantic Avenue
Boston, MA 02106
617-973-3800

Chicago

230 South LaSalle Street
Chicago, IL 60690
312-322-5369

Cleveland

1455 East Sixth Street
Cleveland, OH 44101
216-579-2000

Dallas

2200 North Pearl Street
Dallas, TX 75201
214-922-6100

Kansas

925 Grand Blvd.
Kansas City, MO 64198
816-881-2409

Minneapolis

250 Marquette Avenue
Minneapolis, MN
612-340-2075

New York

33 Liberty Street
55480 New York, NY 10045
212-720-6619

Philadelphia

100 North Sixth Street
Philadelphia, PA 19105
215-574-6675

Richmond

701 East Byrd Street
Richmond, VA 23261
804-697-8000

St. Louis

411 Locust Street
St. Louis, MO 63101
314-444-8703

San Francisco

101 Market Street
San Francisco, CA 94105
415-974-2330

New issues of Treasuries are sold by the government at regular, publicly announced auctions. Older issues, on the other hand, are sold through stockbrokers in what is known as the "secondary market."

Call 202-874-4000. You'll get a recorded message with information on how to buy Treasuries by mail. There's also a listing of other important data and telephone numbers. Hang on until the end and there's a live person to answer your specific questions.

Pamphlets and material on Treasuries is available from:
> Bureau of the Public Debt
> Consumer Services
> Washington, DC 20239-0001

✚ **Help!**

Basic Information on Treasury Bills, Notes, Bonds (free)
> Federal Reserve Bank of New York
> Issues Division
> 33 Liberty Street
> New York, NY 10045
> 212-720-6619

Buying Treasury Securities at Federal Reserve Banks ($4.50)
> Federal Reserve Bank of Richmond
> Public Affairs/Research
> PO Box 27471
> Richmond, VA 23261

U.S. Financial Data ($21/year; weekly newsletter)
> Federal Reserve Bank of St. Louis
> PO Box 66953
> St. Louis, MO 63166

Bond Basics

Before we go any further, let's find out how bonds actually work. This information applies to bonds issued by the U.S. Treasury, by corporations, and by municipalities.

Simply stated a bond (unlike a stock) is an IOU. When you purchase a bond you are, in effect, lending your money to the issuing company or government agency. Bonds come in three types:

1. Those issued by the U.S. Government and its agencies
2. Those issued by corporations
3. Those issued by states, town, or municipalities, known as tax-exempt or "munis"

The issuers of the bond are obligated to pay back the full purchase price at a particular time and not before. This is called the **maturity date**.

In general, bonds fall into two time-related categories: **intermediate notes**, which mature in two to ten years; and **long-term bonds**, which mature or come due in ten years or longer.

Until your bond matures, you will receive a fixed rate of interest on your money. This is called the **coupon rate** and is usually paid out twice a year. For example, on a $1,000 bond that pays 8 percent, you receive a $40 check every six months until maturity.

For trivia buffs: The term "coupon" dates from the time when all bonds actually came with a page of attached coupons. On each specified date, the owner of the bond clipped off the coupon, took it to the bank, and exchanged it for cash.

The **face value** or denomination of a bond is also known as par value and is typically $1,000. That means bonds are sold at $1,000 when first issued. After that, their price will vary, moving up and down just as stocks do.

Depending upon the prevailing market conditions, bonds sell at **either above par** (that is, above $1,000), which is also called **at premium**; or they sell **below par** (that is, less than $1,000), which is called at a **discount**.

And just to make it all a bit more confusing, although bonds are issued and sold in $1,000 units, their prices in the newspaper are quoted on the basis of $100, not $1,000. So you must always add a zero to the published price. For example, a bond quoted at $105 is actually selling for $1,050.

The Secondary Market

After bonds have been issued, they rise and fall in price depending upon supply and demand and upon interest rates. If rates have gone up and new bonds are paying more interest, then older bonds drop in price. On the other hand, if new bonds are paying less interest, then older bonds rise in price—they are seen as being more desirable.

You can sell your bond before its maturity date in the secondary market through a stockbroker—but bear in mind that it's possible you will not get back what you paid for it, particularly if rates have gone up.

Buying Treasuries

Treasures are first sold through auctions held periodically by the U.S. Treasury. The auctions are held primarily for major bank and government bond deals, however the public may participate, too. (We'll tell you how in a bit.) These large buyers determine the final interest rate; in other words, no one knows what rate a Treasury issue will pay until the end of the auction.

How You Can Join the Auction

Most people find it simplest to buy Treasuries through a broker and pay the $25 to $50 bond fee. Yet there's no need to pay this fee—you can also buy Treasuries at the government auctions, either through the mail or in person from the Federal Reserve Bank in your area. When you do, there's absolutely no fee involved.

There are 12 Federal Reserve districts, each with a main bank and 36 additional branches. (See the list on page 93.)

Dates for Treasury auctions are always announced in advance—check the financial section of your newspaper or other publications. You can also call your area's Federal Reserve office and find out. Auctions tend to be monthly, although recently the government has been scheduling fewer of them.

When you call your Federal Reserve Bank, you'll be given taped information about how to place a bid, or many banks will send you a brochure describing the process. You'll need to fill out an order form, known as a tender. It's about one page long and you'll need to fill in your name, address, and Social Security number. Your bank will explain how you can pay. Be prepared: You'll probably need a cashier's check or a certified personal check.

You will also be asked for a "routing number." This is the nine-digit number that appears on the lower left of your personal bank check. The Treasury needs this number so it can deposit the interest and final principal payments directly into your bank account.

When you complete the form (be sure you sign and date it), send it to your Federal Reserve bank or branch, or if you live in the Washington, DC area to: Bureau of Public Debt, Securities Transaction Branch, Washington, DC 20239-1001.

The Treasury Direct System

All sales of Treasuries are electronically recorded on a "book-entry" basis through what is called the Treasury Direct System. You will not get a certificate showing ownership of your Treasury as was the case in the dark ages before computers.

There's one problem with the Treasury Direct System—it is designed for those who plan to hold their securities until maturity.

➤ **Hint:** If you need to sell before maturity, you must transfer your Treasuries out of the Treasury Direct System and into the commercial book-entry system. To do this, set up an account with a stockbroker or a bank that will sell them for you. You'll have to pay a fee. To transfer your T-bills or notes, you must fill out form PD5179, "Security Transfer Request," available from any Federal Reserve Bank or branch.

➤ **Hint:** If you know you will not be holding your Treasuries until they mature, buy them from a broker. This automatically puts you in the commercial book-entry system from the beginning.

Note: You don't have to wait until an auction to buy Treasuries: You can purchase them in the secondary market (described above). Just call several brokers and find out what their fee is. Many discount brokers also handle Treasuries.

PART FIVE

When You Have $5,000

16

Bonds: Corporates, Munis, and Zeroes

"Gentlemen prefer bonds," noted Andrew Mellon. And so should women and children.

In Chapter 15 we discussed U.S. Treasury notes and bonds as the ultimate, safe choice if you want steady income. There are two other types of bonds that also offer income: **corporate bonds** and **municipals.**

Corporates pay slightly higher rates than Treasuries, but they're also higher in risk. On the other hand, municipal bonds, whose yields are lower, have a great tax advantage: Their interest is exempt from income tax at the federal level and, in many cases, at the state and local levels as well.

Both corporate and municipal bonds pay a set rate of interest twice a year for the life of the bond, and if you hold the bonds until maturity, you'll get back the face value—$1,000 per bond.

Most brokerage firms require a minimum of at least $5,000 or $10,000 to buy bonds. With your $5,000 you will be able to purchase five bonds, which is not sufficient diversification to protect you against default and calls. At the $5,000 level, it's wiser to purchase a unit investment trust or bond fund; both are explained below.

However, in preparation for the day when you have $10,000 or more, let's take a look at how to find high quality bonds.

How to Select Bonds

Using Credit Ratings

Before purchasing a corporate or a municipal bond, take a minute or two to find out about the issuer's credit-worthiness as reported by either Standard & Poor's or Moody's—the two leading independent rating services.

Both services periodically update their rating and publish them in huge volumes available at most public libraries and brokers' offices.

BOND RATINGS		
Moody's		**S&P's**
Aaa	Top quality	AAA
Aa	Excellent	AA
A	Very high	A
Baa	Medium	BBB
Ba	Speculative	BB
B	Lower speculative	B
Caa	Poor and risky	CCC
Ca	Near default	CC
C	In default	C

The highest rating a bond can receive is triple A. Medium-grade bonds fall into the triple B category, while those that are C or lower are speculative. In general, inexperienced and conservative investors should stick with bonds rated A or better.

A bond's yield also reflects the issuer's credit quality. Lower quality bonds, also known as noninvestment grade—those rated BB or below—generally have higher yields than better quality, safer issues. The higher yield compensates the investor for lending money to a company that is considered somewhat likely to default on its interest or principal payments.

In addition to the credit risk or financial shape of the corporation or municipality, there are two additional risk factors to bear in mind when investing in bonds: interest rate risk and the call factor, or recall risk.

- **Interest rate risk** is a problem only if you sell your bonds prior to maturity. If interest rates have climbed since your purchase, your bond may very well be worth less than when you bought it. That's because newly issued bonds, paying the new higher rates, are more prized. Of course, the opposite is also true: If rates fall, your bond will be worth more because it is still paying the old higher rate. Solution: Hold bonds until maturity.
- **Recall risk.** Believe it or not, your bonds may actually be "called in," which means they'll be taken away from you prior to maturity. This is something many investors are unaware of. Not all bonds can be called, but those that can have what is known as a "call feature." This gives the issuer the right to redeem the bond before maturity.

  You receive the full face value of the bond, but you then face the problem of investing that money at the prevailing rate, which is usually lower than the one you were receiving.

How to Know if a Bond Will Be Called

The conditions for calling in a bond are provided in the statement filed with the SEC when the bonds are first issued to the public. Call features are also listed in the bond guides.

The call feature is usually not exercised if the current interest rate is the same as or higher than the bond coupon rate. But if interest rates fall below the bond's coupon rate, the bond may be called because the issuer can now borrow money at a lower rate. The issuer, in fact, may decide to take advantage of the lower rates and issue a new series of bonds. (Remember, a bond is just a loan you make to the issuer, who would naturally prefer to pay the lowest interest rate possible.)

Protecting Yourself

If a bond is called in, you then lose that steady stream of income you thought you had locked in for a given number of years. But there is a way to protect yourself from calls, which is essential when investing long term. You can buy a bond with "call protection." This guarantees that the bond will not be called for a specific number of years. Corporate bonds are likely to offer ten-year call protection. Most government bonds are not callable at all, but check carefully— contrary to popular belief, some are.

↗ **Hint:** Check with your broker to find out if a bond has call protection.

Corporate Bonds

Thousands of U.S. corporations raise money by selling bonds to the public. Some of these companies are small and obscure; others are well known. In general, it is best to stick to the bonds of leading companies and those that are traded on the New York Stock Exchange. Then if you need to sell, you can do so more easily than if you owned thinly traded bonds.

Bond prices are listed in the financial pages of the newspaper. They are quoted with fractions listed in eighths. For example, a bond listed at $98-1/4 sells for $982.50.

Here's what a typical listing looks like:

Bond	Current Yield	Sales in $1,000	High	Low	Last	Net Change
duPont 6 1/2 06	6.97	39	93 3/8	92 3/4	93 1/4	+1/8

The first column indicates that this E.I. duPont Corporation bond has a coupon rate of 6.5 percent and a maturity date of 2006. In other words, it pays $65 per year for every $1,000 bond, and it will do so until the year 2006.

If you divide the coupon rate (6.5 percent) by the current market price (listed under "Last" and in this example is $93 1/4), you will get the current yield (6.97 percent).

The volume of bonds traded was 39. The high was $93.375 and the low $92.75. The closing price was $93.25, up $12.50 per bond.

You may wonder why the yield for the bond rose from 6.5 percent to 6.97 percent. The reason is that the price of the bond has gone down from $1,000 on the first day issued to $932.50.

Should You Buy Corporate Bonds?

Yes—if you stick with top-rated, financially solid corporations such as Xerox, IBM, duPont, Eastman Kodak, Bristol Myers Squibb, and the sounder public utility companies. You will achieve a steady flow of income for the life of the bond.

Another advantage that corporate bonds offer is that they can be used in your IRA, SEP, or Keogh plan—plans that defer taxes on earnings.

But remember, unlike Treasury bills, notes, and bonds, corporate bonds are not guaranteed or backed by the government. Corporate bond issuers can and have defaulted. Your protection is the financial strength of the corporation. And the greater the financial strength of the issuer, the lower the coupon or interest rate because safety is traded off for lower yields.

➦ **Hint:** If you live in a high-tax state, factor in the tax advantage of Treasury issues when considering corporate bonds. Income earned on Treasuries is subject to federal income tax but not state and local taxes.

A Corporate Bond Portfolio

- General Electric 7.17 percent coupon, due 1998
- Exxon 6.5 percent coupon, due 1998

- Commonwealth Edison 8.75 percent coupon, due 2005
- Dow Chemical 8.5 percent coupon, due 2005
- Bell Tel of PA 8.25 percent coupon, due 2017

↗ **Hint:** The owner of these bonds will receive his or her return of principal staggered over three different years, starting in 1998 and ending in 2017. This technique, called **laddering**, can also be done with CDs. It is particularly effective for meeting college tuition bills, retirement needs, or other specific financial goals.

Corporate Bond Mutual Funds

As we mentioned above, with $5,000 you can buy only five bonds, and thus shares in a corporate bond mutual fund is a wiser choice. In a mutual fund you will own a proportionate part of a larger number of bonds, and the portfolio is professionally managed.

Three suggestions:

- Fidelity Short Term Bond Fund 800-544-8888
- T. Rowe Price Short Term Bond 800-638-5660
- Vanguard Short Term Bond Fund 800-662-7447

Municipal Bonds

Municipal bonds, also known as tax-exempts, are a good choice for anyone in the 28 percent or higher tax brackets. "Munis," as they are called on Wall Street, are issued by cities, counties, states, and special agencies to finance various projects. Their biggest plus: Interest paid is exempt from federal income tax and, to residents of the area where issued, state and local taxes.

🛑 *Caution:* Two tax traps: 1) If you buy municipals outside the state where you are a resident, their interest incomes will be subject to taxes in your state. And 2) any capital gains made when you sell municipals is subject to all federal and most state tax laws.

Because of their tax advantage, municipal bonds pay lower interest rates than comparable corporate bonds or government securities.

The major retail brokers such as Merrill Lynch, Paine Webber,

CORPORATE BONDS

For Whom

- Anyone seeking high fixed income who also accepts the risk of changing interest rates
- Best for those who can hold their bonds until maturity in order to get back the bond's full face value

Safety Factor

- Can be determined by bond ratings with AAA and AA being the highest
- Varies depending upon the corporate issuer
- Are not insured or guaranteed

Minimum Investment

- $1,000 (many brokers have a $5,000 minimum)

Advantages

- Corporate bonds almost always pay higher interest rates than government bonds or those issued by municipalities
- You can select bonds to come due when you need an influx of cash
- A sound way to get a steady stream of income

Disadvantages

- Many bonds have call provisions
- If you sell before maturity you may get back less than you paid
- Interest income is subject to federal, state, and local taxes
- There is generally minimum appreciation of your principal, whereas with many stocks, investors benefit from significant increases in the price of their shares

and others are primarily interested in working with customers who have a minimum of $15,000 to $25,000 to invest in these bonds.

Although you may indeed find a regular broker, or a discount one who will take smaller orders, the commission will be hefty vis-à-vis your dollar investment. And markups on munis sold through brokers range from 1 to 4 percent.

So, if you have $15,000, invest instead by purchasing a unit investment trust or municipal bond fund, explained below.

Tips for Selecting Tax-Exempt Bonds

There are three factors to check when considering tax-exempt bonds: safety, yield, and liquidity. You can check the safety of any bond, tax-exempt or not, through Moody's or Standard & Poor's rating services.

SAFETY

In addition to sticking to A-rated bonds, you can increase your safety factor by purchasing bonds that are insured even though their yields are slightly lower than uninsured munis. Because municipal bond issuers have occasionally defaulted—the best known example being the Washington Public Power System—insured bonds are a sound idea in today's economic climate.

In order to insure a bond, the issuer pays an insurance company a premium that ranges from 0.1 percent to 2 percent of the bond's total principal and interest. The insurance company agrees to pay both the principal and the interest to bondholders if the issuer defaults on making payment. Policies generally last the life of the bond. Your broker can tell you which bonds are insured. For additional information on insured municipal bonds, write to:

AMBAC Indemnity Corp.
1 State Plaza
New York, NY 10004
212-668-0340

YIELD

The second factor in municipal bond selection is yield. Tax-exempts, as we mentioned before, pay lower interest rates than most taxable bonds, and therefore are not appropriate for people in low tax brackets or for placement in already tax-deferred retirement accounts, such as an IRA. Yet for investors in high tax brackets, municipal bonds can reap surprisingly good returns.

If, for example, you are married, file a joint return, and earn $45,000 annually, you need a yield of 10.76 percent on a taxable investment such as a corporate bond to equal a 7.75 percent tax-exempt yield. The chart on page 113 shows the relationship between taxed and tax-free income.

➤ **Hint:** You can further boost your return by investing in triple-exempt municipals—those in which interest is free from federal, state, and local taxes for residents. Triple-exempts are especially good for people living in states with high income taxes.

LIQUIDITY

The third factor involved in municipal bond selection is liquidity—that is, the ability to find someone who wants to buy your bond, should you wish to sell before maturity. It is best to stick with bonds of large, well-known municipalities or state governments. If you want to sell an obligation of the Moorland Iowa School District, for example, it may be weeks before you find a dealer willing to buy these obscure bonds.

Note: Municipal bond mutual funds are also very liquid.

Types of Municipal Bonds

- **General obligation bonds (GOs)** are the safest category of munis. Sold to help build roads, schools, and government buildings, they are tax-exempt as long as no more than 10 percent of their proceeds goes to a private enterprise. Bonds issued for nonprofit organizations are also tax-exempt. GOs have the highest safety ratings because they are backed by the issuer's full taxing and revenue-raising powers.
- **Revenue bonds** depend upon the income earned by a specific project or authority, such as road or bridge tolls, or revenues from a publicly financed hospital.
- **Industrial development bonds** are issued to finance facilities that are in turn leased to private corporations. The tax law

stipulates that if more than 10 percent of the proceeds raised by their sale is used by private enterprise, the interest a bondholder receives may be subject to a special tax, known as the alternative minimum tax (AMT). The AMT is designed to make sure that Americans with tax-sheltered investments do not escape paying income taxes.

STOP *Caution:* Before investing in an industrial development bond, check with your accountant to see if you are subject to the AMT. If so, avoid these particular bonds.

Hint: Zero coupon municipals are an excellent way to save for a child's education. They are sold at a discount and redeemed in the future at a higher face value. And you never have to pay federal income tax on them. Zeros are explained in full at the end of this chapter.

Municipal Bond Mutual Funds and Unit Investment Trusts

As you know, putting all your eggs in one basket is not sound planning. As a hedge against the risk of an issuer defaulting, it's wise to hold at least five to ten different bonds and/or buy only insured bonds.

Here are three reasonably priced ways to own a diversified muni bond portfolio with just $5,000. In all three, your risk is spread out through participation in large, diversified portfolios of bonds that are professionally selected.

Municipal Bond Mutual Funds

A municipal bond fund's portfolio is made up of tax-exempt munis; most hold over 100 bonds. The typical minimum investment is $1,000. They operate like any other mutual fund. The portfolio manager buys and sells securities in order to maximize the fund's yield. Unlike a unit investment trust (explained below) in which the yield is fixed, a mutual fund's shares fluctuate on a daily basis.

Interest earned is automatically reinvested unless you give directions to the contrary, and an increasing number of bond funds allow you to write checks, usually a minimum of $500, against the value of your shares.

If you ever wish to sell, the fund will buy back your shares at the current market price.

Tax-Exempt Unit Investment Trusts

For those who wish to lock in a fixed tax-exempt yield, a unit investment trust is ideal. Most require a minimum investment of $1,000 per unit. These prepackaged, diversified portfolios lock in a specific, unchanging yield. Unlike bond mutual funds, they are

---

FIVE MUNICIPAL BOND MUTUAL FUNDS

Alliance Municipal Insured National, 800-221-5672
Benham National Tax Free Intermediate, 800-345-2021
Flagship Tax-Exempt Limited Term, 800-227-4648
Scudder Medium Term Tax-Free, 800-225-2470
Vanguard Muni High Yield, 800-662-7447

"unmanaged," and once the bonds for the trust have been selected, no new issues are added. (Issues that turn out to be a problem, however, can be sold in order to minimize losses.) The trust gradually liquidates itself as the bonds mature.

Unit investment trusts are set up by big brokerage houses and bond dealers who buy several million dollars worth of bonds and then sell them to individual investors in $1,000 pieces. You pay the broker a one-time up-front fee, commonly 4.5 percent. You also pay trustee fees of up to .2 percent a year.

A typical unit investment trust holds 20 bonds until maturity, unless the bonds are called or defaulted. Most hold bonds maturing in 25 to 30 years, though some are set up to end sooner, and you can buy them with shorter maturities in the secondary market.

Note: While you own a trust, you receive tax-free income on a monthly or quarterly basis.

➤ **Hint:** Don't be surprised if your checks are not the same every month. As bonds mature or are called, this activity is reflected in your monthly checks.

If you do not wish to hold the trust until maturity, you can sell it in the secondary market either to the sponsor or to another broker. What you get back will depend on the market. If interest rates have fallen, you will get more; but if they've gone up, it's possible that you may not even get back your original price.

🛑 *Caution:* Unit investment trusts are not as liquid as mutual funds.

Talk to your broker in order to find out which trusts are available now, and at what price. Be certain to check the rating of the bonds held in trust. For tops in safety or if you're conservative, stick with AAA-rated bonds or buy an insured trust.

Single-State Investment Trusts and Bond Funds

These are a good investment if you live in a high income tax state. Both single-state investment trusts and single-state bond funds contain bonds that have a triple tax exemption—that is, free from federal, state, and local taxes for residents of the issuing state.

Trusts are sold by regional brokers, large brokerage firms, and bond specialists. In addition, two companies sponsor a number of single-state trusts. Contact them for further information:

John Nuveen
312-917-7700
Van Kampen Merritt
800-225-2222

Single-state muni mutual bond funds are sold by the mutual fund company in the case of no-load funds and by stockbrokers in the case of load funds. Among the leading no-loads with single-state muni funds are:

- Benham
- Fidelity
- Scudder
- Dreyfus
- T. Rowe Price
- Vanguard

STOP *Caution:* Single-state muni bond funds obviously lack the diversity of a broadly based national municipal bond fund. If you live in a state with fiscal problems, put no more than one-third of your tax-free portfolio in single-state mutual funds or unit investment trusts.

THE TAX-EXEMPT EDGE

Find your tax bracket on the left, then at the top of the table find the tax-exempt yield. Read down to determine the yield you need on a taxable security to equal the yield on a municipal.

	Tax-Exempt Yield			
Tax bracket	**6.5%**	**7%**	**7.5%**	**8%**
15%	7.64	8.23	8.82	9.41
28%	9.02	9.72	10.41	11.11
33%	9.7	10.45	11.19	11.94

Zero Coupon Bonds

If you will need money for college tuition, retirement, or to meet some other long-term financial goal, zero coupon bonds offer a viable solution. You make a small investment initially and get a large balloon payment in the future.

How Zeros Work

A zero, unlike regular bonds, pays no interest until maturity. To compensate, it is sold at a deep discount, well below the $1,000 standard bond price, and it increases in value at a compound rate so that by maturity it is worth much more than when you bought it. Although this type of bond does not pay interest along the way, you will be taxed annually by the IRS as though it did.

TAX-EXEMPT UNIT TRUST VS. TAX-EXEMPT BOND FUND

Here are the key differences:

- In a tax-exempt unit trust, the portfolio is fixed; no trading activity is conducted after initial bond purchases are made by the trust.
- In a tax-exempt bond fund, investments are continually bought and sold in order to maximize a high tax-exempt income.
- Unit investment trusts are intended to be held to maturity, typically five to thirty years.
- Bond mutual funds can be for long-term or short-term holding.
- Unit trusts provide regular income checks.
- Bond funds provide income when you sell your shares, although monthly interest income can be sent to you or reinvested.

Let's look at an example: A $1,000 zero yielding 6.2 percent matures in 20 years. It's selling for only $85.40. You pay $85.40. Your $85.40 earns 6.2 percent but you don't receive your investment payments. Instead, they're reinvested and earn 6.2 percent as well. After 20 years, your $84.50 will equal $1,000. Interest turns into principal and is paid to you in a lump sum upon maturity.

Note: EE savings bonds are zeroes.

As you can see, with a zero coupon bond you know ahead of time exactly how much money you will have when the bond comes due on a given date.

The Two Types of Zeros

There are two types of popular zeros: U.S. Treasury zeros or muni zeros. The first are issued by the U.S. Treasury while munis are issued by municipalities, states, and other agencies. There are also a handful of corporate zeros but they are very rare.

ZERO COUPON BONDS

For Whom

- Those who know they will need a certain amount of money at a certain time in the future
- Those who can hold bonds until maturity because zeros fluctuate widely in price

Minimum

- Typically between $150 and $450, but varies widely

Safety Factor

- Minimal risk

Advantages

- You know precisely how much you must invest now to get a certain dollar amount on a certain date in the future
- You do not have to be concerned with the reinvestment of interest payments as is the case with regular bonds

Disadvantages

- Yields are a half to one percentage point below ordinary bonds
- The IRS insists that taxes be paid annually on zero coupon bonds just as if you actually received the interest
- You are paying taxes on theoretical interest even though no cash is received until the date of maturity

17

A Stock Portfolio for Beginners

"Buy stocks that go up, and if they don't, don't buy 'em."
—Will Rogers

Easier said than done. Yet even though stocks go down as well as up, many Americans like owning stocks, owning a piece of American industry. Many actually do more than just think about it—over 28 percent of the U.S. population owns stocks.

There are four compelling reasons why at the $5,000 level, you, too, should consider buying stocks:

- Over the long term, stocks outperform bonds and Treasuries
- Stocks offer the possibility of price appreciation
- Stocks offer the possibility of keeping ahead of inflation
- Stocks, especially those paying high dividends, are also a source of income

↱ **Hint:** If you have never owned a stock, read "What Exactly Is a Stock?" in Chapter 8.

Are You Ready for the Market?

Prior to selecting stocks for your own portfolio, you must have money set aside for an emergency. At least three months' worth of living expenses should be safely stashed away in a liquid investment, such as a money market mutual fund, a money market deposit account, or a certificate of deposit. Once this has been accomplished and you have accumulated $5,000, you're ready to go.

Although it is possible to invest in the market with smaller amounts of money, in order to establish a truly diversified portfolio you need a base of about $5,000. (See Chapter 8 for information on Mini-Investor Plans.)

First determine your investment goals. Are you seeking a stock that pays a high cash dividend, or would you prefer to buy one that will appreciate substantially in price? Do you want liquidity—that is, the ability to get money back when you want it—or are you content to wait for long-term growth? Your goals make a difference, because no one stock offers high dividends, instant liquidity, spectacular appreciation, plus stability.

The Risk Factor

Before you invest, keep in mind that while many stocks are profitable investments and return handsome rewards in terms of capital appreciation, they also can decline in price. There is no guarantee that you will make a profit. Careful selection is essential.

The ABCs of Stock Selection

As you recall from Chapter 8, a **common stock** is a fractional share of ownership in a corporation. For example, if a corporation has one million outstanding shares and you buy one share, you then own one-millionth of that corporation.

This ownership enables you to participate in the fortunes of the corporation. If the corporation prospers, its earnings (which are expressed as earnings per share) will rise, which in turn tends to

117

make the price of the stock rise. Simply put, the corporation's value has increased. Often, a portion of these earnings is shared with stockholders in the form of a cash dividend that is paid out four times a year.

If you believe that certain corporations or industries will flourish in the coming years, try selecting several common stocks in these areas as an investment for income, growth, or a combination of the two.

↗ **Hint:** You might want to follow this rule of thumb, especially at the outset. Don't put more than 10 percent of your money into the stock of any one company and no more than 20 percent in any one industry.

Remember that stocks can also decline in price and you should try to confine your selections primarily to blue chip companies, that is, large, well-financed, and established corporations with secure positions within their industry.

Here are five key standards to use in judging a stock.

1. **Earnings per share should show an upward trend over the previous five years.** If, however, earnings declined for one year out of five, this is acceptable, provided the overall trend continues to rise.

   Earnings per share, simply defined, is the company's net income (after taxes and money for preferred stock dividends) divided by the average number of common stock shares outstanding. You will find it listed in the company's annual report or in professional materials such as *Value Line* or Standard & Poor's *Stock Guide*, available at your library or in any broker's office.

2. **Increasing earnings should be accompanied by similarly increasing dividends.** You should study the cash dividend payments over the previous five-year period. In some cases a corporation will use most of its earnings to invest in future growth and dividends may be quite modest, and rightly so. But even in these cases, some token dividend should be paid annually. Ideally, a company should earn at least $5 for every $4 it pays out.

In conjunction with the company's dividend, you should note its **yield**, which is the current dividend divided by the price of a share. It is listed in the newspaper along with the dividend and other statistics. The yield should be higher for a stock you purchase for income than for one selected for potential price appreciation (see sample stock listing, later in this chapter).

3. **Standard & Poor's rates each company's financial strength.** For you, the $5,000 investor, the minimum acceptable rating should be A.

4. **The number of outstanding shares should be at least 10 million.** Marketability and liquidity depend upon a large supply of common stock shares. Ten million shares ensures activity by the major institutions, such as mutual funds, pension funds, and insurance companies. Institutional participation helps guarantee an active market in which you and others can readily buy and sell the company's stock.

5. **Study the company's price to earnings ratio (P/E ratio).** This ratio is found by dividing the previous year's earnings per share (or the current year's estimated earnings) into the current price of the stock. The **P/E ratio** is one of the most important analytical tools in the business. It reflects investor opinion about the stock and about the market as a whole. For example, a P/E of 11 means investors are willing to pay 11 times earnings for that stock. A P/E of 11 indicates greater investor interest and confidence than a P/E of 7 or 5.

A P/E ratio under 10 is considered conservative, and, depending upon the company, its industry, and your broker's advice, you can feel comfortable with a P/E of 10 or less. As a company's P/E moves above 10, you begin to pay a premium for some aspect of the company's future.

Yet a P/E ratio above 10 may very well be justified by outstanding prospects for future growth, by new technological advances, or by worldwide shortages of a product that the company produces.

Basically, the P/E ratio is the measure of the common stock's value to investors. A low P/E of 5 or 6 usually means

- Sound industries that provide basics—food, drugs, utilities. These tend to hold their own even during recessionary periods.

- Companies that are industry leaders; they can compete.

- Companies that have overseas earnings.

- Companies that do not have heavy debt loads.

- Companies whose products or services you understand.

- More than one company and more than one industry. If you invest in one company and it turns out to be a disaster, you lose everything.

that the prospects are clouded by uncertainty. Similarly, a P/E of 14 or 15 indicates a keen appetite on the part of investors to participate in that company's future.

→ **Hint:** Whatever stock or stocks you decide to buy, you want to get in at the lowest possible P/E—before there is a lot of investor interest and the P/E is bid up. No one can say exactly what ratio you should accept, and it is here that your selection process and your broker's advice become important.

How to Read a Financial Page

Once you own stocks, you will want to know how they are doing—whether they are going up or down in price. To find out, you can read the market quotations in the daily newspaper.

You will find your stock listed under the name of its exchange— the New York Stock Exchange, American Stock Exchange, over-the-counter, and so forth. Here's how it works, using IBM (International Business Machines Corporation) as an example (prices are quoted in fractions of a dollar, so 107 $5/8$ means $107.675 per share):

52 Week		Stock	Div	%	Yield ratio	P/E 100s	Sales			
High	Low	Stock	Div	%	ratio	100s	High	Low	Last	Chg
$123^1/_8$	$93 \, ^1/_8$	IBM	4.84	4.5	15	26586	109	$104 \, ^5/_8$	$107 \, ^5/_8$	$+2 \, ^1/_4$

- The first two columns give the highest and the lowest prices per share for the previous 52 weeks. In the case of IBM, they are 123 $^1/_8$ and 93 $^1/_8$.
- The next column gives an abbreviated form of the stock's name. Here it is IBM.
- Then comes the annual dividend, if any. For IBM it's $4.84.
- Following the dividend is the stock's yield, which is given as a percentage. To determine the yield, divide the dividend by the closing price: $4.84 divided by $107.675 = 4.5 percent.
- After the yield comes the P/E ratio or price divided by earnings. You will note that earnings are not listed in the paper. The P/E here is 15.
- The number 26586 in the next column indicates the number of shares traded that particular day. It is listed in hundreds, so 2,658,600 shares of IBM were traded on that day.
- The next two numbers, 109 and 104 $^5/_8$, tell how high and how low the stock traded that day. In other words, during the course of the day, some stock traded as high as 109 and some trades were made for as little as 104 $^5/_8$ per share.
- The next column shows the price of the final trade that day, and the final column illustrates the change in the closing price from the prior day. In this case it was 107 $^5/_8$, which was 2 $^1/_4$ (or $2.25) over the preceding day's closing price. Sometimes there will be a minus sign, indicating it fell in price. If there's no plus or minus sign, then the closing price was the same as the day before.

Note: These figures do not include the broker's commission.

Buying Stocks

Once you have decided to become involved with the stock market, the next issue to resolve is whether to use a broker or to select your own stocks. Generally speaking, if you have never owned a stock before, it is probably more prudent to get help from an experienced professional than to go it alone.

On the other hand, you could join an investment club (see Chapter 9) or pick hometown stocks (see Chapter 12) and very likely be quite successful.

Selecting a Broker

Knowing when and how to seek the advice of an expert is a critical part of being a successful investor. If you've never had a broker (or if you've had one you did not like) you can find the right one by doing some investigative work well in advance. Plan on spending three to four weeks to locate the broker who is right for you.

Start by thinking about how you selected your doctor or lawyer. Someone else probably suggested them to you. Getting the recommendations of friends and colleagues whose judgment you respect is one of the best ways to find a good broker. Ask your boss, accountant, banker, uncle, or your pediatrician if they have a broker they like.

After gathering several names, call and make appointments with each one. Tell them the amount of money you have to invest. Not all brokers are interested in small accounts, yet many are. Those who are realize that a small account obviously has the potential of becoming a larger one over time. A number of the major "full service" houses, such as Merrill Lynch, Paine Webber, and Lehman Brothers, are indeed willing to open small accounts. Merrill Lynch has a special program for small investors, described on pages 46–48. You will also find that reliable regional brokers are prepared to handle accounts of all sizes, and they are eager to help local investors.

If you feel you don't need investment advice, you can save on commissions by buying through a "discount" broker, such as Charles Schwab, Quick & Reilly, Muriel Siebert, and Olde. In either event, a broker must execute the final buy or sell transaction for you.

Before you interview your broker candidates, prepare a list of questions to ask them. It should include these four items, plus anything else that concerns you:

1. *Do you handle accounts of this size?* You definitely don't want to use a broker who is uninterested in $5,000.
2. *Can you give me one or two references?* Skip over any broker who says no.
3. *How long have you been a broker?* Any broker tends to look great in a good market. You want an experienced person who knows how to handle money in bad times as well as good.
4. *How should I invest my $5,000?* Beware of the broker who advises you to put it all in one stock, or even all in the market. Unless you have specifically said the total amount is to be invested in stocks, the broker should advise you to diversify.

Going It Alone

Once you have gained some feeling for the market, you may want to plunge right in and do your own stock selection.

The best way to minimize risk, of course, is to be well informed. To be your own broker you must be prepared to spend a significant amount of time reading about the economy and about individual companies, as well as the major industries.

Finding Top-Notch Information

- **Specialized financial periodicals and newspapers** are excellent sources of information on the general economic climate and the stock market. In particular, among the newspapers: *Barron's*, *The Wall Street Journal*, *The New York Times*, and *The Chicago Tribune*. Good magazines are: *Forbes*, *Business Week*, *Your Money*, *Fortune*, *U.S. News & World Report*, and *Money*.

    The money section of *USA Today* is excellent for beginners, as is *Better Investing*, the monthly magazine of the National Association of Investment Clubs. Devoted to investment education, it analyzes stocks and covers various views on investments (see Chapter 9).

- **Brokerage firms** have a wealth of research material. The large houses will send you some material, even if you are not a customer—at least for a limited period. Many have copies of newsletters on display in their retail offices. Although much of this information is generally known, you can still gather ideas, and certainly it is valuable for background data.

- **Annual reports of corporations** are an important source. Write or call any company you are considering investing in and ask for a copy. Then read the section in this book called How to Read an Annual Report in the Appendix.

- **Standard & Poor's *Stock Reports*** is regarded as a bible in the financial world. It covers each company listed on the NYSE. S&P also publishes similar volumes for the American Stock Exchange and for over-the-counter stocks. The material is revised periodically. For each corporation you will find a summary description, the current outlook, and new developments, plus a ten-year statistical table.

- **Standard & Poor's *Stock Guide*** is a small monthly booklet containing basic data in condensed form on 5,000 stocks: price range, P/E ratio, dividend history, sales, an abbreviated balance sheet, earnings, and the S&P rating. A similar monthly booklet is put out covering bonds. For further details on all S&P publications, contact:

  > Standard and Poor's Corporation
  > 212-208-8000 or 800-221-5277

- **Value Line Investment Survey** contains the most comprehensive coverage of stocks. Value Line follows 1,700 companies and their industries. Each industry is updated quarterly. Stocks are ranked on the basis of timeliness for purchase and safety. A subscription to this service also includes a separate weekly analysis of the market and general economic situation plus an in-depth discussion of one stock recommended for purchase. Contact:

  > Value Line, Inc.
  > 800-833-0046 or 212-907-1500

- **Financial newsletters can be helpful**, but they vary enormously in reliability and success as far as their advice goes. Before subscribing to any newsletter, try to locate copies at your library or by contacting the publisher. Many will send a free copy or offer trial subscriptions at a reduced rate.

  ➴ **Hint:** There is also a service that rates the advisers. *Hulbert Financial Digest* is a monthly newsletter that tracks and ranks around 100+ of the stock market newsletters based on their performance in recommending stocks. One issue is free; a year's subscription is $59. Contact:

  > *Hulbert Financial Digest*
  > 316 Commerce Street Alexandria, VA 22314
  > 703-683-5905

- **Insider trading.** The sale and purchase of a company's stock by officials of the corporation is one way to determine trends in the price of the stock. This information is given in *Value Line*.

A Beginner's Portfolio

Abbott Laboratories
Bank of New York
Bristol-Myers Squibb
Clorox
CSX Corp.
Emerson Electric
General Electric
Gillette
Heinz
Kellogg
Merck
Mobil Corp.
Procter & Gamble
Smucker's
Time Warner
Wrigley

Companies That Have Paid Dividends
50 Years or More

American Brands
American Home Products
Bristol-Myers Squibb
Duke Power
Dun & Bradstreet
DuPont
Florida Progress
J.P. Morgan
Kmart
Kansas City P&L
Peoples Energy
Potlatch Corp.
Stanley Works
Washington Gas & Light

Companies That Have Increased Dividends
Each of the Last Ten Years

Bristol-Myers Squibb
Campbell Soup
Clorox
Coca-Cola
General Electric
Johnson & Johnson
Kimberly-Clark
Merck
Pfizer
Reuters Holdings
Universal Foods
Wilmington Trust

THE SMARTY'S SIX STEP GAME PLAN

1. Figure out whether you're investing for income or for long-term appreciation, then select stocks that match your goal.
2. When you're investing long term, remember that the market fluctuates by the minute. Focus on earnings, not on daily prices.
3. Know something about the industry. Don't purchase a medical technology stock or a high-tech issue if you don't know about medical technology or high tech.
4. Read the company's annual and quarterly reports before buying its stock. You wouldn't buy a car without a test drive.
5. Stick with companies that are leaders within their industry.
6. Be patient. Think long term, but sell when you've doubled your money.

Your Investment Achilles Heel

Even with rational research and thoughtful planning on your part, you may still fall prey to one or more of the ubiquitous emotional traps that lie in wait in the investment field.

Every investor has areas of vulnerability. If you recognize yours, it's possible to eliminate many errors and reduce misjudgments. Here are the five most common pitfalls you should avoid when buying and selling stocks.

1. Holding on to securities too long, hoping a poor performer will turn around and be a winner. It's rare; learn when to give up.
2. Reacting immediately to negative news and selling too soon. Think about it overnight, then respond.
3. Refusing to sell and take the profit because you feel you can squeeze out a few more points. This is known as greed; resist it.

4. Refusing to take a profit because of capital gains tax, even when the stock is fully valued. This is silly, if not stupid.
5. Avoiding selling a stock you inherited because of sentimental feelings. Really! Stocks have no feelings.

To avoid these five pitfalls, and others, you should set up a smart game plan—based on knowing what your financial objectives are and then sticking to them. Read on. . .

Appendices

A

Using Your Computer

If you have a computer and a modem, you may want to take advantage of the on-line services that provide everything from basic information such as current stock prices, to more detailed information, including earnings and fast-breaking news about corporations.

If you have America Online, CompuServe and/or one of the Net browsers you'll find plenty of options. For up-to-date information on what else is available on-line, check out computer magazines that regularly review the best services and financial advisers.

You should also call several of the discount brokers, such as Schwab, Olde, and White. Many have reasonably priced on-line arrangements for trading as well as for information. These three and others advertise regularly in the financial magazines and business sections of major newspapers.

Some Software Samplings

Software can make money management and investing a lot simpler. Best bets:

- *Microsoft Money.* Great for keeping track of your checkbook and budget; does calculations automatically.

- *Quicken*. Easy to learn and use. Sorts financial information into budget and tax categories for record-keeping.
- *Moneycounts*. A flexible program that handles cash, checking, savings, investments, and even credit card transactions.
- *Andrew Tobias's Managing Your Money*. The most comprehensive financial program with checkbook and portfolio management; also has a calendar to-do list and a tax planner. Calculates mortgage payments and whether to buy or lease things, such as a car or house.
- *Turbotax*. Helps you determine what documents to keep track of, what IRS forms to use, with useful sample worksheets. Easy to read and use.

B

Seven Steps Toward College Tuition

You know college is going to be an expensive proposition, whether your child or grandchild goes to an Ivy League school or to a more reasonably priced state university. There's no need to panic, but on the other hand, there is a need to do something. In fact, there may be several somethings.

Here are seven steps to help you get headed in the right direction.

1. **Call T. Rowe Price** and get a free copy of "The College Planning Kit." It's easy to follow and will help you determine how much money you need to set aside each month, depending upon the age of your child. **Info:** 800-638-5660.

2. **Decide in Whose Name.** If you save funds in your child's name, the interest and earnings, up to $1,300 per year, will be taxed at the child's rate, which is most likely lower than yours. At age 14 all the child's investment income is taxed at the child's rate. (*Note:* these figures are continually adjusted.)

   However, if college savings are in your name, your child

is more likely to get financial aid. Schools ask parents to contribute 5.65 percent of their assets for each year's tuition but require a whopping 35 percent of the assets held in a child's name.

Best bet: Discuss with a knowledgeable accountant before making this decision.

3. **Stockpile EE Savings Bonds.** If you put the bonds in your name and use them to pay for tuition (not room and board), you will escape paying federal taxes on the income the bonds earn. (EE Bonds are exempt from state and local taxes for everyone. See Chapter 3.)

🛑 *Caution:* This works only if your annual adjusted gross income falls below certain caps, currently $93,450 for married couples and $57,300 for single parents. However, these figures will increase along with inflation. Info: 800-US-BONDS.

4. **Fund Your 401(k) Plan.** This and other retirement plans often let you borrow up to 50 percent of the amount invested, or $50,000, whichever is less. The interest rate is typically prime plus one or two points and repayment is made through automatic payroll deductions back into your own account, not to a bank.

5. **Buy Zero Coupon Bonds.** These are tailor-made for college accounts because you know exactly how much you'll get when the bonds mature. Sold at a deep discount, they pay no interest until maturity. For example, a ten-year zero Treasury bond selling for $530 will be worth $1,000 in the year 2005. (See Chapter 16.)

6. **Ladder Back CDs and Treasuries.** Buy a series of CDs and/or U.S. Treasuries timed to come due each fall as your child heads off to school. (See Chapters 7, 15, and 16.)

7. **Consider a Mortarboard Mutual Fund.** Twentieth Century Giftrust Investors Fund is a no-load fund designed to help finance a child or grandchild's undergraduate degree. It buys

stocks of growth companies and has a ten-year compounded annual return of about 23 percent. Your account is set up as an irrevocable living trust, which means you can buy shares only in someone else's name and that someone cannot be your spouse. Your initial investment cannot be withdrawn for at least ten years or until the beneficiary reaches age 18 or 21. **Info:** 800-345-2021.

C

Nine Easy/Painless Ways to Save

Granted, it's much more fun to spend money on a romantic restaurant dinner or on a Caribbean vacation than to save your pennies or dollars. Yet to make certain you can always dine out and travel in style, you do need to save.

Extra dollars not only make dreams come true, they also let you sleep at night. If you want college for your kids, a house of your own, and a retirement nest egg, then build your savings by following these nine easy tips. You'll find saving is infectious.

1. **Make savings your first bill.** Once a month when you pay your bills, write a check to deposit in your money market fund or savings account at your bank or credit union. Start by saving 1 percent of your take-home pay the first month; then increase the amount by 1 percent each month. By the end of the year you'll be socking away 12 percent a year.

2. **Use automatic savings plans.** If you don't see it you won't spend it. Arrange for a certain amount—it can be as little as $50—to be taken out of your paycheck and automatically

transferred to your savings or money market fund at a bank or credit union. Ask if your employer also has an automatic plan for **EE Savings Bonds**. Alternatives: Have your bank automatically transfer a certain amount from checking to savings each month; or have a mutual fund automatically withdraw money from your checking account and put into its highest yielding money fund.

3. **Leave credit cards at home.** Pay with cash or by check. You'll spend less and you'll avoid those whopping monthly interest charges on unpaid credit card balances.

4. **Defer taxes.** Money in an IRA, Keogh, 401(k), or other qualified retirement plan grows tax-free until withdrawn. You can fund these plans by making small contributions several times a year rather than trying to pay in one large lump sum. Alternatives: Buy investments that are fully or partially tax-exempt: municipal bonds, municipal bond mutual funds, EE Savings Bonds, and U.S. Treasury securities. (But don't put them in your retirement plan.)

5. **Contribute to a stock purchase plan.** Many companies allow employees to contribute part of their salary to buy the firm's stock through automatic payroll deductions.

6. **Reinvest stock dividends.** See page 45 for details.

7. **Keep making payments.** When you've paid off a mortgage or a loan, continue to write a check for the same amount (or at least half the amount) every month and put it into savings. You've learned to live without that money, so now you can sock it away.

8. **Save your change at the end of the day.** Small amounts add up quickly. Put your nickels, dimes, and quarters in a jar before going to bed. Better bet: Save one-dollar bills.

9. **Treat yourself.** Saving is smart but not always immediately gratifying. The payoff is sometimes several years away. So spend a little on yourself now and then. It will make saving much easier.

I'd like to leave you with these final words of wisdom from the great mystery writer, Agatha Christie: "Where large sums of money are concerned, it's advisable to trust nobody."

The same is true of small sums, from $50 to $5,000. And, now that you've read this book, you are well armed to trust yourself when it comes to things financial.

Index

About the Author

Nancy Dunnan is a financial analyst. She participates in a call-in program on public radio in New York and appears frequently on CNN. In addition to *How to Invest $50 to $5,000*, she is the author of *Dun & Bradstreet Guide to $Your Investments$*, *Never Call Your Broker on Monday*, and *How to Make Money Investing Abroad*. She writes a monthly column, "Question & Answers," for *Your Money* magazine.

Dunnan was awarded the Distinguished Service Award in Investment Education from the Investment Education Institute, an affiliate of the National Association of Investors Corporation. A native of Ft. Dodge, Iowa, she lives in Manhattan, on a budget.